THE
APOCALYPSE

A READING OF THE REVELATION OF JOHN

Charles H. Talbert

WESTMINSTER JOHN KNOX PRESS
Louisville, Kentucky

Quotations from the Bible are from the Revised Standard Version, second edition, or are by the author unless otherwise specified. Quotations from the Pseudepigrapha are normally taken from James M. Charlesworth, ed., *The Old Testament Pseudepigrapha,* 2 vols. (Garden City, N.Y.: Doubleday, 1983, 1985). Citations from Greek and Roman authors are either from the Loeb Classical Library or are by the author.

Book design by Publishers' WorkGroup
Cover design by Drew Stevens
Cover illustration: Dante Alighieri *by Szabo Béla*

First edition

Published by Westminster John Knox Press
Louisville, Kentucky

This book is printed on acid-free paper that meets the American National Standards Institute Z39.48 standard. ∞

PRINTED IN THE UNITED STATES OF AMERICA

94 95 96 97 98 99 00 01 02 03 04 — 10 9 8 6 5 4 3 2 1

Library of Congress Cataloging-in-Publication Data

Talbert, Charles H, date.
    The Apocalypse : a reading of the Revelation of John / Charles H.
Talbert. — 1st ed.
        p.   cm.
    Includes bibliographical references and index.
    ISBN 0-664-25363-6 (alk. paper)
    1. Bible. N. T. Revelation—Commentaries.   I. Title.
BS2825.3.T255   1994
228'.07—dc20   94-8681

To
the memory of Dale Moody
who taught me to love the scriptures

CONTENTS

PREFACE

The motivation for undertaking this little volume is pastoral. My aim is twofold: to offer aid to those who are scarred by harmful readings of Revelation and to encourage mainstream Christians to deal with the Apocalypse in ways other than ignoring it.

My indebtedness for this book is great. First, I owe thanks to Dr. Jeffries M. Hamilton, Editor of Academic and Reference Books for Westminster John Knox Press. Without his gracious invitation to do a book on Revelation, I would never have undertaken such a project. Second, thanks should go to my colleague, Dr. Fred Horton, who allowed me to teach his course on Jewish and Christian Apocalyptic during the spring semester, 1993, as an aid to my research. Without that opportunity, I could not have completed the project. Third, I owe my greatest debt to the twenty-eight students in the course who accepted my challenge to help me write this volume. Some are named; some are not. All have been my teachers.

My view of the duty of an expositor of scripture is that expressed by Calvin in the preface to his commentary on Romans: "lucid brevity." Whether or not I have achieved this goal, the reader will have to decide.

1

GETTING STARTED

The book of Revelation, of all the books in the New Testament, has had the most checkered history of reception by the church. The following sketch is illustrative.

INTERPRETATION

The Ancient and Medieval Church

By A.D. 200 the Apocalypse was accepted by most mainstream Christians in the Mediterranean world. By that date it was regarded as authoritative in Syria (Theophilus of Antioch, so Eusebius, *Church History*, 4.24); in Asia (Melito of Sardis, so Eusebius, 4.26); in Italy (Justin Martyr, *1 Apology* 28; *Dialogue* 81); in Gaul (Irenaeus, *Against Heresies* 5.30); in Egypt (Clement of Alexandria, *The Instructor* 1.6; *The Miscellanies*, 3.18); and in North Africa (Tertullian, *Resurrection of the Flesh* 27; *Against Marcion* 3.14, 24).

In spite of this overwhelming acceptance, Revelation always had its detractors. From the earliest times it was rejected by Marcion, who thought it was too Jewish (so Tertullian, *Against Marcion* 4.5; 3.14); by the Alogi, who believed its view of the afterlife was too worldly (Irenaeus, *Against Heresies* 3.11.9; Epiphanius, *Medicine Chest* 51.3.33); by Gaius, who thought it heretical (Eusebius, *Church History* 7.25.1–2; 3.28.1–2); by Cyril of Jerusalem (*Catechetical Lectures* 4.36); and by the Syriac Peshitto. Eusebius of Caesarea (*Church History* 3.24.18; 3.25.4) and Jerome (*On Psalms* 149) likewise both had qualms about it. Nevertheless, by A.D. 1300 Revelation had been accepted by virtually all Christians except the Nestorian Church.

The Century of the Reformations

The Council of Trent in A.D. 1546 pronounced the Apocalypse canonical for Roman Catholics. The Thirty-nine Articles accepted Revelation as scripture for Anglicans. The Protestant reformers Luther and Zwingli, however, denied Revelation functional canonical status. Calvin, moreover, wrote commentaries on twenty-six New Testament books but not on Revelation.

Today

The Greek Orthodox lectionary omits Revelation altogether. Catholic and Protestant lectionaries have only minimal readings from the Apocalypse. The book of Revelation is appealed to mostly by fringe groups and figures. The reasons for its marginal status among mainline Christians today are primarily three: (1) the apparent inaccessibility of its meaning; (2) the seeming impossibility of its pastoral application; and (3) its demonstrated susceptibility to abuse.

This volume will argue that (1) Revelation is understandable when read alongside other documents of the same type from antiquity, (2) when so read it has pastoral value and special relevance to the contemporary church, and (3) when read and interpreted properly, it is less susceptible to misuse than when neglected by mainstream Christians and left to less responsible others to interpret.

A fresh reading of Revelation is needed for mainline Christians. Such a reading must start at the beginning. This involves asking certain key questions: (1) Who wrote this document? (2) To whom? (3) From where? (4) For what social function? (5) Using what genre? (6) When? (7) For what purpose? Finding answers will be more difficult for some of these queries than for others. Answers must be attempted for all.

AUTHORSHIP AND SOCIAL PURPOSE

Authorship

Revelation 1:1–2, 4, 9 says that the author was one John. In the ancient church this was interpreted in two very different ways by those who accepted the authority of the Apocalypse. Some held that this John was the apostle, the son of Zebedee, one of the Twelve (Justin, *Dialogue* 81; Tertullian, *Against Marcion* 3.14.24; Hippolytus, *On the Antichrist* 25–26). Others believed it was the elder John who wrote Revelation (Dionysius of Alexandria [so Eusebius, *Church History* 7.25.7–27]). Among those who rejected its authority, some held it was written by the heretic Cerinthus (the Alogi [so Epiphanius 51.3.4]; Gaius [so Eusebius 2.25; 7.25]). All that the document itself says is that the author was one John, an early Christian prophet (1:3; 10–11; 22:9, 18–19).

With the birth of the Christian movement came a rebirth of prophecy. Early Christians, filled with the Holy Spirit, spoke for God or the Risen

Christ (1 Thess. 5:20; 1 Cor. 11:4; 12:10, 28–29; 13:2, 8; 14; Rom. 12:6; Acts 11:27; 13:1–3; 15:32; 19:6; 21:9–10; Eph. 2:20; 3:5; 4:11; Didache 11:3–12; 13:1–7; 15:1–2; Eusebius, *Church History* 3.5). There were two types of early Christian prophets: (1) church prophets who worked primarily in one location (e.g., 1 Cor. 11, 14) and (2) wandering prophets who were itinerant (Acts 11:27–30; Didache 11–13).[1] The John who wrote the Apocalypse was probably not a settled community prophet but a wandering prophet who was familiar with all seven churches because he had visited each. On occasion the problem of false prophecy and prophets arose (Matt. 7:15–23; 1 John 4:1–2). So in Revelation the author of the Apocalypse regards himself as a true prophet who is opposing false prophets (e.g., 2:20). The John who wrote the Revelation was an early Christian prophet who was apparently part of a larger group of prophets in his region (Rev. 22:9—"your brethren the prophets"). Beyond this the internal evidence does not take us.

Recipients

Revelation 1:4 tells us that the prophecy was sent to the seven churches in the province of Asia (2:1, Ephesus; 2:8, Smyrna; 2:12, Pergamum; 2:18, Thyatira; 3:1, Sardis; 3:7, Philadelphia; 3:14, Laodicea).

From Where

Revelation 1:9 says that John wrote from the island of Patmos. He was on Patmos because of "the word of God and the testimony of Jesus." Pliny tells us that at the time Patmos was a penal colony (*Natural History* 4.12.23). Such tiny islands were regularly used by the Romans as places of exile for certain types of prisoners (Tacitus, *Annals* 3.68; 4.30; 15.71; Juvenal, *Satires* 1.73; 6.563–64; 10.170). The early fathers believed the prophet John had been exiled there because of his Christian witness (Clement of Alexandria, *Who Is the Rich Man Who Will Be Saved?* 42; Origen, *On Matthew* 16:6; Tertullian, *Prescription of Heretics* 36; Acts of John 14; Eusebius, *Church History* 3.18, 20, 23; Victorinus, *On the Apocalypse* 10.11). Tertullian claims that John's banishment was of the type called *regulatio in insulam* (*Prescription* 36). This variety of exile involved loss of neither property nor rights. It could be pronounced by a provincial governor, if a suitable island for exile was in his province. It was different from *deportatio in insulam*, a penalty that involved loss of property and civil rights, which only the emperor could impose.

For What Social Function?

Revelation is a script for an oral performance in a ritual setting. That is, it was meant to be read aloud (Rev. 1:3—"Blessed is the one who reads aloud the prophecy"), to be heard (Rev. 22:18—"everyone who hears the words of the prophecy of this book") by Christians (Rev. 1:4, 11; 22:6, 16) in a service of worship (1:10; 22:20). By means of an oral enactment, the auditors entered into another universe and experienced a new reality.[2] Revelation's power continues to be felt best when it is heard.

GENRE

Revelation 1:4–6 says that the author intends to write a public, pastoral letter to the seven churches in the province of Asia and that he understands the content of this letter to be "words of prophecy." In Revelation one finds prophetic/apocalyptic visions within an epistolary framework. The visions belong to a literary genre known as apocalypse. Just as Jewish apocalyptic circles understood themselves in terms of prophecy (4 Ezra 12:42; 14:22; 1 Enoch 81:5–7; Jub. 32:21–16), so John's "words of prophecy" fit nicely into the apocalyptic genre.

Apocalypse is a genre in which a revelation is given by God, to a human seer, through an otherworldly mediator, disclosing future events and/or transcendent reality,[3] which is intended to affect the understanding and behavior of the audience.[4] In some apocalypses this revelation is given to the human seer while he is on a heavenly journey; in others the human receives revelation while still on the earth; in still others both patterns are found together. Given this definition, pseudonymity is not an essential trait of an apocalypse.[5] Revelation, The Shepherd of Hermas, the Book of Elchasai, and Hippolytus's *On Christ and Antichrist*, for example, are four Christian apocalypses that are not pseudonymous.

There is extant a considerable body of Jewish apocalyptic writings:[6] for example, 1 Enoch 1–36 (ca. 200 B.C.); Daniel 7–12 (160s B.C.); 1 Enoch 85–90, the Animal Apocalypse (160s B.C.); Jubilees 23 (second century B.C.); 1 Enoch 93:1–10; 91:11–17, the Apocalypse of Weeks (first or second century B.C.); Testament of Levi 2–5 (first or second century B.C.); 1 Enoch 37–71 (early first century A.D.); Testament of Moses (early 1st century A.D.); 2 Enoch (late first century A.D.); 4 Ezra (end of first century A.D.); 2 Baruch (ca. A.D. 100); Apocalypse of Zephaniah (first or second century A.D.); Apocalypse of Abraham (first or second century A.D.); Testament of Abraham (first or second century A.D.).

A sizeable body of early Christian writing exists that also falls into this genre:[7] for example, Mark 13 (first century A.D.); 2 Thessalonians 2 (first century A.D.); Shepherd of Hermas, "Visions 1–4,"(late first or early second century A.D.); Didache 16 (late first or early second century A.D.); Ascension of Isaiah 6–11 (late first or early second century A.D.); Apocalypse of Peter (second century A.D.); 5 Ezra 2:42–48 (second century A.D.); Book of

Elchasai (second century A.D.); 6 Ezra 15–16 (third century A.D.); certain Christian portions of the Sibylline Oracles (e.g., Sib. Or. 8.194–216, 217–500 [second century A.D.]; Sib. Or. 7 [second century A.D.]). The best preparation for reading the Revelation to John with understanding is first to read through these Jewish and early Christian apocalypses.[8] After such a reading exercise, the Apocalypse of John seems much less the strange world it did before such a reading.

Exposure to a large number of these apocalypses allows one to draw some distinct conclusions about the literature. First, Apocalypses contain an apocalyptic eschatology. Apocalyptic eschatology is the belief that the judgment of the wicked and the vindication of the righteous entails the destruction of the world and the resurrection of the faithful to a blessed heavenly existence.[9]

Second, apocalyptic writings arise out of multiple social situations. They sometimes come out of a social crisis and are the product of the marginalized in society (Daniel 7–11; 4 Ezra) but not always.[10] Some reflect speculative thought (e.g., 1 Enoch 72–82; Apocalypse of Peter), and some by no means reflect the marginalized (e.g., Testament of Abraham; Shepherd of Hermas).

Third, the goal of apocalyptic is often hortatory. Among pagan apocalypses, both the Myth of Er (Plato, *Republic* 10.614B–621B) and the Dream of Scipio (Cicero, *De Republica*, the last book, known through the commentary on it by the fourth-century A.D. scholar Macrobius) have a clearcut ethical aim. In 2 Esd. 14:11, 13 is found clear evidence from a Jewish apocalypse. The angel says this to Ezra:

> For the age is divided into twelve parts, and nine of its parts have already passed (11). . . . Now therefore, set your house in order, and reprove your people, comfort the lowly among them, and instruct those that are wise (13).

The Shepherd of Hermas, "Visions," 1–4, among Christian apocalypses reflects the same purpose. In 4.2.5 we read:

> Go then and tell the Lord's elect . . . that this beast is a type of the great persecution which is to come. If then you are prepared beforehand and repent with all your hearts . . . you will be able to escape it, if your mind be made pure and blameless, and you serve the Lord blamelessly for the rest of the days of your life.

Like prophecy, apocalyptic writing often aimed to change the behavior of its audience.

Fourth, apocalyptic literature employs certain compositional techniques in its writing: for example, symbolism, numerology, formalized surface structure, and recapitulation. Each needs attention if understanding is to be attained.

Apocalypses are written with a high level of symbolism. Apocalyptic writings are addressed to the imagination. Their intent is more to create an emotional impression than to give new information.

> The language of the apocalypses is not descriptive, referential newspaper language, but the *expressive* language of poetry, which uses symbols and imagery to articulate a sense or feeling about the world. Their abiding value does not lie in the pseudoinformation they provide about cosmology or future history, but in their affirmation of a transcendent world.[11]

The symbolism serves this end. The symbols should not prevent understanding in any serious way. Some symbols are explained by the writer (e.g., Rev. 1:20 tells the reader that the seven lampstands are the seven churches of Asia; Rev. 12:9 explains that the great red dragon is the devil; Rev. 17:18 says the woman drunk with the blood of the saints is the great city). Other symbols are not explained in any explicit way but are self-explanatory to those acquainted with the Old Testament (e.g., the tree of life, Rev. 2:7; 22:2, comes out of Gen. 2:9; 3:22–23; the rod of iron, Rev. 2:9, comes from Ps. 2:9); with apocalyptic literature generally (e.g., the lake of fire, Rev. 19:20—cf. 1 Enoch 67:13; the great white throne, Rev. 20:11—cf. 1 Enoch 25:3); and with the general cultural background (e.g., the woman clothed with the sun, Rev. 12:1, 2, 14—cf. the pictures of Isis in antiquity [Apuleius, *Metamorphoses* 11.3–4] and the Jewish image of the Messiah's coming as a birth from the community [1 QH 3:4]). Sometimes the meaning of the symbols is not obvious. Then one has to interpret the unclear by the clearer. (Comparison of the measuring of the temple, Rev. 11:1–2, for example, with the sealing of the 144,000 in Rev. 7:3–4 indicates that both refer to divine protection of God's people during the tribulation.) Failure to take the highly symbolic character of apocalyptic into account virtually guarantees a misreading of the text.

Revelation also reflects the symbolic use of numbers in antiquity.[12] The number 1 conveys the idea of uniqueness or independence. Number 2 stands for doubling of energy, strengthening, confirmation (Rev. 11:3). Number 3 is a symbol for the divine (Rev. 1:4–5) or its counterfeit (Rev. 16:13). The number 3½ indicates a limited time, a time with an end (Rev. 12:14). Number 4 is the cosmic number, derived from the four corners of the earth (Rev. 7:1; 21:13). Number 6 stands for incompleteness and, therefore, evil. When it is raised to 666, it points to the ultimate in imperfection and evil (Rev. 13:18). The number 7 is the most sacred number. It expresses completion, 4 (the earth) + 3 (the divine) (Rev. 1:11; 6:1; 8:6; 15:1). To use seven of anything raises it above the level of the particular to the level of the general or universal. So the letters to seven churches represent more than just communication with a number of particular congregations in Asia; they refer to the church on earth. The numbers 10 (2 x 5) and 12 (4 x 3) also express fullness. When 12 is multiplied by 12, the result is perfect fullness (Rev. 7:4); also when 10 is multiplied by 10, the result indicates a great expanse of time (Rev. 20:2). In a document in which numbers are used extensively in this way, it is a misreading to take them otherwise. (For example, when Rev. 17:10–12 uses seven, five, and ten of kings, it is to be taken as a symbolic statement of completeness in each case, not as an enumeration of a historical line of rulers.) The numbers in Revelation cannot be understood by assigning them real numerical value, not even as round numbers. They are purely symbolic.

Apocalyptic often uses a highly formalized surface structure. For example, the Jewish apocalypses, 4 Ezra and 2 Baruch, are both organized into seven visions.[13] Revelation is similar in its use of the number seven in its overall arrangement. The Apocalypse opens with seven letters to seven churches (2:1–3:22). There follow seven cycles of revelations: (1) 4:1–8:1; (2) 8:2–11:18; (3) 11:19–13:18; (4) 14:1–20; (5) 15:1–16:21; (6) 17:1–19:5; and (7) 19:6–22:5. Each begins with a vision of some heavenly reality that functions to give Christians assurance in the face of what follows.[14] Five of the seven visions themselves are organized around the principle of seven (6:1–8:1, seven seals; 8:6–11:18, seven trumpets; 14:6–20, seven angels of judgment; 16:1–21, seven bowls of wrath; 19:11–22:5, seven visions of the end). The other two are each organized around five scenes (12:1–13:18 and 17:1–19:5). Recognition of these principles of organization assist reading comprehension of what is otherwise a very difficult book to understand.

The seven visions of the end times found in Revelation do not move forward in chronological order so that what is narrated in cycle two (8:2–11:18) or cycle four (14:1–20) is necessarily later in time than the events recited in cycle one (4:1–8:1). Instead, Revelation follows the principle of recapitulation. The seven visions go over the same subject matter but with variations. This has been recognized at least since Victorinus of Pettau (ca. A.D. 270). It can already be seen in the visions of Daniel 7–12. There the subsequent visions (chap. 7; chap. 8; chaps. 10–12) do not move forward in time but rather advance in clarity and detail the same message. The succeeding visions recapitulate the basic point of the first but with variations. In so doing apocalypses followed the rules of Mediterranean rhetoric. (*Rhetorica ad Herrennium* 4.42.54 says: "We do not repeat the same thing precisely—for that, to be sure, would weary the hearer and not elaborate the idea—but with changes.")

Recapitulation is a characteristic of argument by means of narrative. If one uses analytical logic to construct an argument, then one might argue, "On the one hand," followed by "On the other hand." If, however, one uses a narrative to make the argument, it is done by repetition. The first time through in telling the story one makes the "On the one hand" argument; in the second run-through of the story, one makes the "On the other hand" point. Argument is done by repetition with variation.

In terms of ancient Mediterranean ways of thought, it is a way of thinking in totalities. As J. Schildenberger puts it:

> As a consequence of the Hebrew's thinking in totalities, it is easy to see that in presenting his subject-matter, the Hebrew does not develop it so much in logical order, step by step from general to particular, but rather from the out-set he has the complete topic concretely in mind, and not being able to present it all at once, he keeps coming back to it, letting it be seen from various aspects, now emphasizing this angle, now that, until in the end the full picture, which we saw totally but not clearly from the very start, has been imbibed with full grasp and satisfaction.[15]

In terms of modern information theory, this is redundancy. In literary works, redundancy aims to make it increasingly difficult for the reader to make a mistake. The repetition aims to make sure the message gets through all the "noise" of extraneous signals that may mislead.[16] Only as readers take account of the symbolism, the symbolic use of numbers, the formalized surface structure, and the practice of recapitulation can they expect to move toward understanding when reading the Revelation to John.

DATE

In the ancient church there were four dates offered for Revelation: (1) the time of Caligula (A.D. 37–41) and Claudius (A.D. 41–54) (Epiphanius 51.12.32–33); (2) the time of Nero (A.D. 54–68) (Syriac versions);[17] (3) toward the end of Domitian's reign (A.D. 81–96) (Irenaeus, *Against Heresies* 5.30.3, who is followed by many others);[18] and (4) during the reign of Trajan (A.D. 98–117) (Theophylact on Matt. 20:22; Dorotheus). How should this diversity of opinion be evaluated?

The first two options seem impossible for several reasons. First, Polycarp, *To the Philippians* 11, says that the church at Smyrna did not exist during the time of Paul (died ca. A.D. 64). Second, since Revelation knows the myth of Nero's return (Rev. 13:3; 17:11), it is post–A.D. 68, the date of Nero's death. Third, since Rome is called Babylon in Revelation, apparently because she has destroyed Jerusalem just as Babylon had centuries before (2 Kings 25; 2 Esd. 3:1–2, 28–31; 2 Bar. 10:1–3; 11:1; 67:7; Sib. Or. 5.143, 159; 1 Peter 5:13), the Apocalypse must be post–A.D. 70. In Rev. 11:1–2, the temple is only a metaphor for the church and is, therefore, not useful for dating purposes.

Between the last two dates suggested by the ancients it is difficult to decide. Sometimes Revelation has been dated to the 90s because of a link with an alleged persecution of Christians by Domitian. Whether there was a widespread persecution of Christians under Domitian is irrelevant for dating the Apocalypse because Revelation does not reflect either a past or a present great persecution but rather a future tribulation (Rev. 2:10; 3:10) much like that in the Shepherd of Hermas, "Visions," 1–4 (also written probably in the 90s). Indeed, the similarities between Revelation and Hermas in this regard could be used as an argument for a common date in the 90s. A complicating factor is the claim of the Alogi (Epiphanius 51.33.1) that the church at Thyatira did not exist during the lifetime of John the Apostle. A major problem here is whether the Alogi believed John the apostle died in the middle of the first century or at the beginning of the second. When all is said and done, all that is required is that Revelation be written in time for Papias to know it (A.D. 140s). We are reading, then, a document from either the end of the first or the beginning of the second century.

PURPOSE OF THE
BOOK OF REVELATION

Why was Revelation written? In current discussions three main answers are given to this question.

1. The first maintains that Revelation is persecution literature. It was written because of a persecution under Domitian and designed to be a call to endurance in the midst of suffering. This has been the traditional answer of New Testament scholars in the twentieth century.[19] Two problems challenge one's confidence in this answer. First, it is not certain that Domitian was a persecutor of the church in Asia. Eusebius calls Domitian a persecutor of the church, but he offers only a couple of stories to support the claim, neither of which applies to Asia (*Church History* 3.17–20, 39). The Roman authors who condemn Domitian say nothing about a persecution in Asia (Pliny the Younger [*Panegyrics* 2.33.4; 52.7]; Suetonius ["Life of Domitian," 13:2]; Dio Chrysostom [*Orations* 1.22–24; 45.2; 50.8]; Dio Cassius [*Roman History* 67.4.7; 67.13.4; 67.8.1; 67.14]). There is, further, no convincing evidence that Domitian pursued the emperor cult in any way greater than did his predecessors. Based on the evidence at hand, one must conclude that there is no evidence of state-sponsored persecution of Christians in Asia during the time of Domitian.[20]

The situation of Christians in Asia during the time of Domitian and Trajan was the same. Pliny reflects the situation about A.D. 110 in Bithynia (*Epistle* 10.96).

This is the practice I have used in the case of those brought before me as Christians. . . . The usual consequence followed; the very fact of my dealing with the question led to a spread of the charge, and a large number of cases were brought before me. An anonymous notice was posted, containing many names. Those who denied that they were or had been Christians I thought should be discharged, because they called upon the gods using the formula provided and did reverence, with incense and wine, before your image which I had ordered to be brought forward for this purpose. . . . and especially because they cursed Christ. It is said that genuine Christians cannot be induced to do such.

The Emperor Trajan responds (Pliny, *Epistle* 10.97):

You have taken the right line, dear Pliny, with regard to the cases of those denounced as Christians. There is no hard and fast rule of universal application that can be laid down. Christians are not to be sought out. If they are accused and the charge is proved, they are to be punished, but with this reservation: if any one denies that he is a Christian, and actually proves it by worshipping our gods, he shall be acquitted.

Pliny's letter indicates that only after the larger populace had accused Christians of crimes did the governor intervene. Worship of the emperor was required only of those accused of a lack of loyalty.

This is basically the same Roman practice as that followed just after A.D. 70 in Egypt. Josephus (*War* 7.10.1 § 407–19) tells that when the Jews of Alexandria handed over to the Romans their Jewish kinsmen, the Sicarii, who had fled thither after the revolt in Palestine, the latter were called upon to confess Caesar's lordship. For Christians, then, normally it was the pagan mob that was the problem, not the state. Indeed, the later martyrdom of Polycarp indicates how on imperial feast days mob violence toward Christians was regarded as an expression of loyalty to the emperor.

A second challenge to the Domitian persecution literature theory is that Revelation speaks about a great persecution to come, not about one already being experienced (2:10; 3:10).[21] Indeed, there is only one martyr known to the prophet John (2:13). The visions of terrible suffering that are depicted in Revelation 6–20 all belong to the future. They are the prophet's projection of what will happen when Rome becomes aware of the incompatibility between its ethos and that of the church.

These two problems, taken together, undermine confidence in the traditional view of the purpose of the Apocalypse, namely, that Revelation is persecution literature aiming to encourage Christians who are suffering because they will not worship Domitian in the emperor cult.

2. A second purpose suggested for Revelation is that it is therapeutic literature written to serve as an emotional catharsis for Christians. Although these Christians were not experiencing persecution, they felt oppressed and harbored strong negative feelings that, if not released in a harmless way, might result in disastrous negative actions.[22] One can only

respond: Neither the text of Revelation nor any other apocalyptic writing, Jewish or Christian, verbalizes such an intent.

3. A third purpose posited for Revelation is that it is anti-assimilation literature addressed to Christians, some of whom advocated accommodation to the pagan culture and some of whom were willing to assimilate to a non-Christian milieu because of their spiritual anemia and lethargy. It functions as a call to radical Christian commitment.[23] Persecution is anticipated by the prophet because his inspiration enables him to see the inevitable clash to come between the ethos of Roman imperial society and that of the Christian community. The two kingdoms are, at root, incompatible. Given this vision of the ultimate incompatibility between Roman culture and Christian values, the church may expect all the force of imperial power to be brought against them. Visions of such anticipated persecution functioned as the ground for a call to single-minded devotion to Jesus in the present, very much like what one finds in the Shepherd of Hermas, "Visions," 1–4.

There, in an apocalypse from Roman Christianity in the 90s, one sees the problem as

> the degeneration of quality of life in a milieu in which many Christians are economically comfortable, upwardly mobile, and inclined to find vigorous fidelity to the demands of religious visionaries uninteresting if not downright threatening. . . . These are not people caught up in world affairs, but rather in the daily events of business-as-usual in the Roman streets.[24]

The overall framework of Hermas, "Visions" 1–4, is that of cosmic eschatology, involving ultimate destruction of the world and divine retribution. In this context, the seer sees a great beast coming toward him. It is interpreted to mean the great tribulation/persecution that is coming upon the Christians. Hermas survives by his single-minded faith. Confronted by such faith, the beast lies down and lets Hermas pass undisturbed. Hermas is commanded to go and tell his fellow Christians that this is the way to survive the great tribulation/persecution that is coming upon them. Here apocalyptic eschatology functions in the interests of spiritual purity, single-minded devotion to God.

It is Hermas who furnishes the closest analogy to what is going on in the book of Revelation.

> The danger that beset John's churches consisted of compromise, cultural accommodation and assimilation, which was all the greater since neither persecution by the state nor abject poverty determined their present.[25]

John's remedy is "first-commandment faithfulness" ("You shall have no other gods besides me," Ex. 20:3). The framework of a future persecution allows the lines between the two kingdoms, that of God and that of Rome, to be drawn in starkest terms. The value systems of the two kingdoms are thereby shown to be mutually exclusive. The Christians' choice must be not "both–and" but "either–or." Such a message is pastorally relevant to our own times, which mirror the prophet's circumstances almost exactly.

Having attempted answers to the questions that constitute a beginning to a fresh reading of Revelation, it is now time to offer an outline of the document that may facilitate a fresh reading.[26]

1:1–8	Letter introduction
1:9–3:22	The call of the prophet and the seven letters to the churches
4:1–22:5	Seven visions of the shift of the ages
4:1–8:1	Opening the seven seals
8:2–11:18	Blowing the seven trumpets
11:19–13:18	The roots and role of Roman imperial power in the sufferings of Christians
14:1–20	Seven angels of judgment
15:1–16:21	Seven bowls of wrath
17:1–19:5	The role and the results of Roman imperial power's part in the suffering of Christians
19:6–22:5	Seven scenes of the consummation
22:6–21	Epilogue

The material from 4:1–19:5 (Visions 1–6) focuses on the period of great suffering that was believed by Jews and Christians alike to precede the shift of the ages, called by such names as "the tribulation," "the Messianic woes," the "birth pangs of the new age," or simply "judgment" (meaning judgment within, but at the end of, history). Material in 19:6–22:5 (Vision 7) focuses on what, in Jewish and Christian apocalyptic thought, comes after the great period of suffering: parousia, last judgment, new heavens and new earth. Taken together, these two foci furnish a vision of the future that lays the groundwork for a call for Christian resistance against assimilation to the idolatrous culture of the state.[27] Before the visions (4:1–22:5), however, come the letters to the seven churches in the province of Asia. To this section (1:9–3:22) we must turn next.

2

THE SEVEN LETTERS TO
THE SEVEN CHURCHES
(1:1–8; 1:9–3:22)

TITLE AND INTRODUCTION
REVELATION 1:1–8

Revelation 1:1–8 is the opening of the document. It consists of the title of the volume (vv. 1–3) and a letter introduction (vv. 4–8).

Verses 1–3 fall into two parts: the title (vv. 1–2) and a blessing (v. 3). Old Testament prophets (Isa. 1:1; Jer. 1:1; Ezek. 1:2–3; Hos. 1:1) and Christian writers alike (Mark 1:1; Epiphanius, *Medicine Chest* 1.1.1) often began with a statement of what their books were about. So the Christian prophet John begins by stating what the book is about (the revelation of Jesus Christ, v. 1a) and how it was communicated (from God to Christ to the angel to John to the churches, vv. 1b–2). What follows is a blessing (the first of seven beatitudes: 1:3; 14:13; 16:15; 19:9; 20:6; 22:7; 22:14) on the one who reads the prophecy aloud in church and on those who hear and heed its message and the reason for the blessing (for the time is near, v. 3).

Verses 4–8 contain the letter introduction: A to B greeting, followed by a prayer form. John writes to the seven churches in Asia. His greeting is a Christianized version: Grace and peace from "him who is and who was and who is to come, and from the seven spirits who are before his throne, and from Jesus Christ the faithful witness, the first born of the dead, and ruler of kings on earth" (vv. 4b–5).

The greeting raises problems of interpretation. Who are the seven spirits before the throne (1:4b; cf. 4:5)? Are they the seven archangels of Jewish thought (Tobit 12:15) who in Rev. 8:2 are said to stand before God? In Rev. 1:16 Christ has in his right hand the seven stars, which are said in 1:20 to be the angels of the seven churches. In 3:1 Christ is designated as the one who has "the seven spirits of God and the seven stars." Are the stars and spirits here synonyms or are they separate entities? Does the reference to the seven spirits refer to the Holy Spirit? Would an incipient trinitarian formula have included angels as its second element? Would the prophet John have regarded archangels as a source of grace and peace?

Is it not better to distinguish between the stars and spirits in 3:1 and regard the seven spirits as Revelation's equivalent to the Holy Spirit? The formulas that elsewhere in the New Testament list God, the Son of Man, and angels alongside one another (Luke 9:26; 1 Tim. 5:21; Rev. 3:5) have a different order, one that lists angels last.

Or are the two conceptions, Holy Spirit and angels, united in some way? In ancient Judaism and early Christianity, "spirit" and "angel" were often used interchangeably (Jewish—1 QM 13:10–11; Jub. 1:25; 15:31–32; 2 Enoch 16:7; T. Abraham 4:18; 9:1–3; Christian—Heb 1:14; Origen, *Against Celsus* 8.64). In one Jewish source, Holy Spirit and archangel seem to be used as synonyms. In the Testament of Abraham 4:15, the Holy Spirit puts into Isaac's mind the thought of death; in 7:22, Michael, an archangel, puts into Abraham's mind the thought of death. In some circles of early Jewish Christianity, the Holy Spirit is called an angel. The Shepherd of Hermas, "Mandate," 11:9, says regarding a true prophet, "the angel of the prophetic spirit rests on him and fills the man, and the man, being filled with the Holy Spirit, speaks to the congregation as the Lord wills."

The Ascension of Isaiah 7:23 refers to the angel of the Holy Spirit; 9:35 says, "I saw the Lord and the second angel" (= the angel of the Holy Spirit who has spoken in Isaiah and in the other righteous); 10:4 speaks of the Lord and the angel of the Spirit; and 11:4 mentions the angel of the Spirit. In both early Christian sources, the angel of the Holy Spirit is the prophetic spirit.

In Revelation the pervasive view of the Holy Spirit is that of the prophetic spirit. To be "in the Spirit" (1:10; 4:2; 17:3; 21:10) refers to prophetic inspiration. The expression "says the Spirit" (14:13b) or "the Spirit says" (22:17) refers to a prophetic word. The expression "to hear what the Spirit says" (2:7, 11, 17, 29; 3:6, 13, 22) means to heed the prophetic message. In Revelation the ultimate sources of the prophetic word are God (22:6) and Christ (1:1; 19:10). The prophetic Spirit's message consists of words of the risen Christ (cf. 2:1 with 2:7; 3:1 with 3:11, etc.). Can it be that we find in Revelation the same primitive Christian pneumatology already found in Hermas and the Ascension of Isaiah? If so, the seven spirits are the Holy Spirit (the completeness of God's spirit) understood in angelic terms (i. e., as God's messenger) as the spirit of prophecy.

Following the greeting in the space usually reserved in letters for a prayer form is a threefold expression of praise. The first is a prayer. "To him who loves us and has freed us . . . and has made us a kingdom . . . to him be glory and dominion for ever and forever. Amen" (vv. 5b–6). The second is a prophecy followed by a responding prayer: "Behold, he is coming with the clouds, and every eye will see him. . . . Even so. Amen" (v. 7). The third is an aretalogy (= a form in which the deity lists his or her virtues): "I am the Alpha and Omega, says the Lord God . . ." (v. 8). Within this letter envelope comes the revelation from Jesus Christ (1:9–22:5). The revelation consists of two main parts: first, the prophet's call and commission followed by seven letters to seven churches (1:9–3:22) and, second, seven visions of the shift of the ages (4:1–22:5). We now turn to the first main part.

PROPHETIC CALL AND THE SEVEN LETTERS
REVELATION 1:9–3:22

This is a thought unit composed of two segments: First is 1:9–20, which contains the inaugural audition (vv. 10–11), vision (vv. 12–16), and commission (vv. 17–20). (For accounts of prophetic calls prior to prophetic oracles, cf. Ezek. 1:1–3:11; Isa. 40:1–11; Jer. 1:4–10.) The second segment consists of seven messages to seven churches in the province of Asia (2:1–3:22). The inaugural christophany (1:9–20) lays the foundation for what follows. Its components are clearcut.

Rev. 1:9–20 = The prophet's call
        Setting (9)
        Audition (10–11)
        Vision (12–16)
        Commission (17–20)

Each must be examined in order.

The setting is the island of Patmos where John, the prophet, is exiled because of his Christian activities (v. 9). Reference to his suffering would lend the prophet credence. Juvenal, *Satires* 6.560–64, writes hostilely about such people:

> Fellows like these are believed if they've been in some far-off prison, shackled hand and foot; if he hasn't a prison record, then he has no renown, but a sentence to the islands, a narrow escape from death, procures for him a reputation.

While in the Spirit on the Lord's Day (= Sunday; cf. 1 Cor. 16:2; Acts 20:7; Didache 14:1; Ignatius, *Magnesians*, 9:1; Melito [Eusebius, *Church History* 4.26.2]; Dionysius of Corinth [Eusebius, *C.H.* 4.23.11]; Clement of Alexandria, *Miscellanies* 7.12; Tertullian, *Chaplet* 3; Gospel of Peter 35 and

50), John experiences an audition. He hears a loud voice commanding him to write what he sees and to send it to the seven churches in the province of Asia (vv. 10–11).

The audition is followed by a vision (vv. 12–16). John turns and sees seven golden lampstands (Zech. 4:2) and in their midst "one like a son of man" (Dan. 7:13). This glorious one is clothed with a long robe (= priestly garments, Ex. 28:4, 27), with a golden girdle around his breast (= royal emblem, 1 Macc. 10:89). He has white hair (= divine appearance, Dan. 7:9), eyes like a flame of fire (= angelic appearance, Dan. 10:6), feet like burnished bronze (= angelic appearance, Dan. 10:6), and a voice like the sound of many waters (= strong, Ezek. 1:24). In his right hand he holds seven stars (cf. 1:20); from his mouth issues a sharp two-edged sword (= the messianic weapon, Isa. 11:4; 49:2; Wisd. Sol. 18:15–16; 1 Enoch 62:2; 4 Ezra 13:10; Psalms of Solomon 17:27, 39); and his face is like the sun at midday (= heavenly radiance, 1 Enoch 14:21; 51:4; 71:1; 89:22, 30). John witnesses an awesome christophany. From it comes his commission.

The prophet's commission comes in vv. 17–20. As is customary in epiphanies (= appearances of the divine; cf. Ezek. 1:28–2:1), John falls down but is restored by a word of reassurance from the risen Christ (vv. 17–18). There follow John's instructions: "Now write what you see, what is and what is to take place hereafter," (v. 19; for divine commissions to write, cf. Pausanias 1.21.2; Aelius Aristides, *Oration* 48:2; Callimachus, *Causes* 1.1.21–24). An interpretation of part of the vision follows ("the seven stars are the angels of the seven churches and the seven lampstands are the seven churches," v. 20). With this, the prophet John's commission is complete. Now he must write to the seven churches as Christ has commanded him.[1]

What follows the prophet's call in 1:9–20 are seven letters containing prophetic oracles (for prophetic oracles in letter form, cf. 2 Chron. 21:12–15; Jer. 29; 2 Baruch 77:17–19, 78–87; Epistle of Jeremiah; 1 Enoch 91–108).[2]

Rev. 2:1–7, to Ephesus
      a. To . . . write . . . from (1)
      b. I know (2–6)
            Praise—2–3, 6
            Censure—4
            Change—5a
            Warning—5b
      c. Let those with ears to hear, listen (7a)
      d. Promise (7b)

The letter to Ephesus follows a stereotyped form. Each part merits attention.

The letter is *to* "the angel of the church in Ephesus" (v. 1). In Revelation, as in Jewish apocalyptic (1 Enoch 90:2; 2 Baruch 55:3; 4 Ezra 4:1; 5:15, 32; 7:1), an angel is a medium of revelation (1:1—He made it known by sending his angel to his servant John; 22:6—God has sent his angel to show his servants; 22:8—the angel who showed them to me; 22:16—I, Jesus, have sent my angel to you with this testimony for the churches). So in Rev. 2:1, 8, 12, 18; 3:1, 7, 14, the angels of the churches are the agents of revelation, those who mediate a divine message to humans. The message mediated is a word of the risen Christ (2:1, 8, 12, 18; 3:1, 7, 14) via the Holy Spirit (2:7, 11, 17, 29; 3:6, 13, 22). John's prophetic word goes to the angels of the seven churches who are to mediate it to the congregations. On this there seems to be little disagreement. The issue is, Who are the angels? Are they the bishops of the churches? the prophets of the churches? guardian angels of the churches? the churches' alter egos? In the context of Revelation, these angels (= messengers) are best understood as the prophetic leadership of their various congregations (22:6). The letter is *from* the risen Christ who holds the seven stars in his right hand and who walks among the seven churches (1:13, 16, 20).

The section beginning, "I know" (vv. 2–6) mingles praise and blame. The praise comes in vv. 2–3, 6: The church does not tolerate the heresy of the Nicolaitans.

> The author of Revelation appears to formulate his theology in opposition to (a) . . . position which advocated accommodation to the syncretistic Roman religion and its cultic practices. Since loyalty to the Roman civil religion did not necessarily involve creedal statements, but mainly required participation in certain cultic acts and ceremonies, enthusiastic theology made it possible to conform to the imperial cult without giving up faith in the one true God and Jesus Christ. . . . it allowed Christian citizens to participate actively in the social, commercial, and political life of their society. This theology, probably represented by the Nicolaitans, . . . advocated . . . a policy of accommodation.[3]

Such accommodation is rightly rejected by the Ephesians.

The censure is found in v. 4: the church has abandoned the love it had at the first. Change is called for (v. 5a—repent), reinforced by a warning (v. 5b—If not, I will come and remove your lampstand = take away the church). An exhortation to heed the prophetic message follows: "The one who has an ear, heed what the Spirit says to the churches" (cf. Mark 4:9, 23; Matt. 11:15; Luke 14:35). The exhortation is undergirded with a promise (v. 7b—To those who conquer [= remain faithful] I will grant to eat of the tree of life [cf. 22:2]).

Rev. 2:8–11, to Smyrna
   a. To . . . write . . . from (8)
   b. I know (9–10)
         Circumstances—9, 10b
         Encouragement—10a, c
   c. Let those with ears to hear, listen (11a)
   d. Promise (11b)

The second letter, this one to Smyrna, follows the same stereotyped form as the first. It is addressed *to* the angel of the church in Smyrna. It is *from* the risen Christ, who is the first and the last (1:17), who died and came to life (1:18). The section introduced by "I know" (vv. 9–10) offers only encouragement to this church. Their circumstances are hard. They are economically poor (v. 9a), the only one of the seven churches so designated; they are slandered by the synagogue (v. 9b; cf. 1 Thess. 2:14–16; Rom. 2:28; Acts 13:45; Justin, *Dialogue* 16:11; 47:15; 96:5; 110, "whose name you profane and labor hard to get it profaned over all the earth"; Tertullian, *Scorpiace* 10); they are about to suffer a time of testing and tribulation (v. 10a). Encouragement is offered: v. 10b—"Be faithful unto death, and I will give you the crown of life" (= the crown which is eternal life; James 1:12; 2 Tim. 4:8; Hermas, "Parable," 8.2.6; Martyrdom of Polycarp 17:1; 5 Esd. 2:43–46; T. Benjamin 4:1). The conventional exhortation to heed what is said (v. 11a) is followed by the customary promise: "The one who conquers (= resists assimilation) shall not be hurt by the second death (vv. 11b; 20:14; Jerusalem Targum on Deut. 33:6—"Let Reuben live in this age and not die the second death whereof the wicked die in the next world").

Rev. 2:12–17, to Pergamum
   a. To . . . write . . . from (12)
   b. I know (13–16)
         Praise—13
         Censure—14–15
         Change—16a
         Warning—16b
   c. Let those with ears to hear, listen (17a)
   d. Promise (17b)

Another stereotyped letter follows, to Pergamum. It is *to* the angel of the church at Pergamum. It is *from* the risen Christ, "who has the sharp two-edged sword" (v. 12; cf. 1:16; 19:15). The section that begins "I know" (vv. 13–16) mingles praise and blame. The praise section (v. 13) recognizes the hardship of their circumstances. They live where Satan's throne is. An altar of Zeus, an Asclepios cult, and a major site of the worship of the Roman emperor were all situated in Pergamum. One, two, or all three would have merited the label "where Satan's throne is." They have persevered even through the martyrdom of one of their members. (Note that this is the only martyr to which the seven letters refer!) The section containing censure is more extensive (vv. 14–15). Some of the members hold the teaching of Balaam (= the teaching of the Nicolaitans): idolatry and immorality. Balaam (Num. 25:1–2; 31:16) had been transformed in post-biblical Judaism into one who seduced Israel with false teaching (Josephus, *Antiquities* 4.6.6 § 126–28; Philo, *Moses* 1.54 § 295–99) the gist of which was take part in the libations and sacrifices offered to other gods in order to participate in pagan society more fully.[4] Repentance is called for (v. 16a), followed by a warning: "If not, I will come to you soon and war against you with the sword of my mouth" (v. 16b).

The customary exhortation follows: "Let those with ears to hear, hear" (v. 17a). It is supported by a divine promise. To those who conquer (= resist assimilation), the risen Christ will give two things: some of the hidden manna that was believed to be stored up for the end times (2 Macc. 2:4–8; 2 Bar. 29:8; Sibylline Oracles 7.148–49) and a white stone with a new name on it (= a new identity given by deity; cf. Aelius Aristides's *Hymn to Asclepios* in which the devotee of the god has a vision during which the deity gives him a token bearing his new name, Theodorus).

> Rev. 2:18–29, to Thyatira
>> a. To . . . write . . . from (18)
>> b. I know (19–25)
>>> Praise—19, 24–25
>>> Censure—20
>>> Change—21–22
>>> Warning—21–23
>> c. Promise (26–28)
>> d. Let those with ears to hear, listen (29)

The fourth of the letters again follows the stereotyped form. It is addressed *to* the angel of the church in Thyatira. It is *from* the Son of God, who has "eyes like a flame of fire (1:14) and whose feet are like burnished bronze" (1:15). The section beginning "I know" (vv. 19–25) mingles praise and blame. The praise comes in vv. 19, 24–25. Not only do the majority in the church hold fast to the faith, but their latter works exceed those at the first (v. 19). They are orthodox and ethical. They should continue as they are (v. 25).

Nevertheless, there is much to censure as well (v. 20). The majority tolerate a female prophet whose teaching leads to immorality and idolatry. She is like Jezebel in the Old Testament (1 Kings 16:31; 2 Kings 9:22) who led Ahab astray and resisted the true prophet, Elijah. Those who commit adultery (= spiritual faithlessness, Hos. 4:10) with her will be thrown into great tribulation (v. 22). This church, with its numerous good works, tolerates heretical teaching. The probable background of this problem lies in the developed trade guild system in Thyatira. These guilds were not only economic; they had a religious basis. When they met, it was often in a pagan temple for a communal meal whose food came from a sacrifice (cf. 1 Cor. 10:19–22). If, in Pergamum, Christians' lives are threatened by the pervasiveness of the imperial cult, here their economic well-being is threatened if their participation in the sacrifices by the guilds is not forthcoming. Apparently the prophetess argued that Christians could join a guild and participate in the feasts without thereby compromising their faith. Christians were initiated into a deeper wisdom (cf. deep things of Satan, v. 24). They knew an idol was nothing, and so they could not be defiled by that which did not exist (cf. the same argument by Paul's opponents in 1 Cor. 8:4, 7a, 8). For the prophet John, however, such participation violated the Apostolic Decree (Acts 15:19–20, 29). The needed repentance would involve repudiation of involvement in the guilds. The issue was simple for John: either assimilation to pagan culture with its non-Christian basis or nonassimilation.

A promise precedes the final exhortation. Those who do not assimilate (= conquer) will receive two benefits: rule over the nations in the end time (vv. 26–27; 20:4; 1 Cor. 6:2) and the morning star (= immortality, Dan. 12:3, or Christ at the parousia, Rev. 22:16). The concluding exhortation reinforces the notion that all this is contingent upon Christian faithfulness (v. 29, those with ears, let them hear).

> Rev. 3:1–6, to Sardis
> > a. To . . . write . . . from (1a)
> > b. I know (1b-4)
> > > Censure—1b
> > > Change—2–3a
> > > Warning—3b
> > > Praise—4a
> > > Promise—4b
> > c. Promise (5)
> > d. Let those with ears to hear, listen (6)

Once again, this letter to Sardis follows the stereotyped form. It is addressed *to* the angel of the church in Sardis; it is *from* the risen Christ "who has the seven spirits of God and the seven stars" (1:20). The section that begins "I know" (vv. 1b–4) is severe. The church is indicted: "You have the name of being alive, and you are dead" (v. 1b). Change is called for: "Awake (= remember what you have received and heard; keep that, and repent, v. 3a). . . . If you will not awake, I will come like a thief, and you will not know at what hour I will come upon you" (vv. 2–3). This echoes events of Sardis's past. According to Herodotus (*History* 1.84), Sardis was captured by the Persian king Cyrus, because the city was not awake. A Persian soldier was watching when a Lydian soldier dropped his helmet over the walls and down the cliff and then made his way down the cliffs, recovered his helmet, and made his way back up again. That night the Persian soldier and a select band of warriors climbed the cliffs the same way. When they reached the top, they found the walls completely unguarded. Everyone was asleep. So the Persians entered unopposed and took the city while its people slept. The same thing happened to the city in another battle two hundred years later. The people of Sardis have always had trouble remaining awake in the midst of danger. If the church at Sardis does not remain spiritually awake, Christ will come upon them at the last judgment like a thief (Luke 12:35–40).

Even though the church as a whole is dead, there are a few individuals who have not soiled their garments (= by accommodation with the cultural environment). Just as Roman citizens wore white togas on special days, especially at a triumph (Juvenal, *Satires* 10.45), so those who have not sold out to pagan culture will walk with Christ in white at his parousia (v. 4). The promises (v. 5) come before the final exhortation. To those who conquer (= do not assimilate) Christ promises white garments at his parousia (= the wedding garment that allows admission into the feast, Matt. 22:11–13), their names recorded in the book of life (= the heavenly book in which the redeemed's names are written so that they are guaranteed a place in God's kingdom; Ex. 32:32–33; Ps. 69:29; Isa. 4:3; Dan. 12:1; Phil. 4:3; 1 Clem. 53:4; Hermas, "Parable," 2:9), and Jesus' acknowledgment before God at the last judgment (Matt. 10:32–33; Mark 8:38). The expected exhortation ends the fifth letter: "Let those with ears hear what the Spirit says to the churches" (v. 6).

> Rev. 3:7–13, to Philadelphia
>> a. To . . . write . . . from (7)
>> b. I know (8–11)
>>> Praise—8, 10a
>>> Promise—9, 10b
>>> Encouragement—11
>> c. Promise (12)
>> d. Let those with ears to hear, listen (13)

The sixth letter continues in the stereotyped form used previously. It is addressed *to* Philadelphia; it is *from* the risen Christ who is "the holy one, the true one, who has the key of David, who opens and no one shall shut, who shuts and no one opens" (Rev. 1:18; 3:7). Just as Eliakim carried the keys of the house of David in the court of Hezekiah (= controlled entry into the king's house, Isa. 22:22), so does Christ in the kingdom of God.

The section beginning "I know" (vv. 8–11) offers only praise and encouragement to the church: "I have set before you an open door" (= an evangelistic opportunity, 1 Cor. 16:9; 2 Cor. 2:12; Col. 4:3). "You have kept my word" (= the word of patient endurance, v. 10a) "and have not denied my name" (v. 8). Two promises are forthcoming. First, "Behold, I will make those of the synagogue of Satan who say they are Jews and are not (= the Jewish synagogue that rejects and opposes Jesus) . . . come and bow down before your feet (as God promised Israel the Gentiles would do to them, Isa. 60:14), and learn that I have loved you" (as God had promised Israel, Isa. 43:4) (v. 9). The roles have been reversed. The Christians are now God's people and, as such, inherit the promises made to Israel. Second, "I will keep you (= protection, not exemption, John 17:15) from the hour of trial which is coming on the whole earth (= the tribulation, 2 Bar. 32:1; 40:2; 71:1; 4 Ezra 9:7–8; Mark 13:8; Hermas, "Visions" 1–4), to try those who dwell upon the earth" (v. 10b). Third, "I am coming soon" (v. 11a). Here is the risen Christ's promise of an imminent end (1:1, 3; 10:6; 12:12; 17:10; 22:6, 7, 12, 20a; cf. 4 Ezra 4:26–27, 44–50; 5:50–55; 8:61; 2 Bar. 85:10; 1 Thess. 4:13–18; Phil. 4:5; 1 Cor. 15:52; Heb. 10:25, 37; James 5:7–9; 1 Peter 4:7; 1 John 2:18; Epis. of Barn. 21:3–4; 1 Clem. 23:5; 2 Clem. 16:3; Hippolytus, *In Daniel* 4.18–19). In the light of such a promise, the Christians are encouraged to "hold fast what you have, so that no one may seize your crown" (of life, 2:10, cf. 1 QS 4:7) (v. 11b).

Again the promise precedes the final exhortation (v. 12). Those who conquer (= do not assimilate) are offered two benefits. First, "I will make . . . pillars in the temple of my God (Gal 2:9); never shall they go out of it (Ps. 23:6)" (v. 12a). Whenever a man served the state well, the memorial the city gave to him was often to erect a pillar with his name inscribed on it in one of the temples. Just so, in God's temple. Second, "I will write on them the name of my God (14:1; 22:4), and the name of the city of my God . . . (21:9–10), and my own new name (14:1; 19:13–16)" (v. 12b). The customary exhortation ends the letter. "Let those with ears, hear. . . ." (v. 13).

Rev. 3:14–22, to Laodicea
        a. To . . . write . . . from (14)
        b. I know (15–20)

Censure—15–17

Change—18–20

c. Promise (21)

d. Let those with ears to hear, listen (22)

The last of the seven letters follows the expected stereotyped form of all the others. It is addressed *to* the angel of the church of Laodicea (Col. 4:13–16); it is *from* the risen Christ, "the Amen ("Yes, so let it be," cf. 2 Cor. 1:19), the faithful and true witness (1 Tim. 6:14), the beginning of God's creation (Col. 1:15; Rom. 8:29)" (v. 14). Here for the first time, the description of the risen Christ is not drawn from the inaugural christophany.

The section that begins "I know" (vv. 15–20) is heavy on censure. "You are neither cold nor hot. Would that you were cold or hot! So, because you are lukewarm . . . I will spew you out of my mouth" (vv. 15–16). Six miles away in Hierapolis there were hot springs. As it made its way over the plateau, the water gradually lost its heat. When it finally poured over a cliff opposite Laodicea, it was lukewarm. The Laodiceans could hardly miss the allusion to the lukewarm water of the springs that made people sick if and when they drank it. Their spiritual condition is likened to this tepid water. Why are they like this sickening drink? It is because they say they are rich and need nothing (= self-sufficient, v. 17a). The church reflects the character of the city at large. Tacitus, *Annals* 14.27.1, records that after a major earthquake, Laodiceans refused Roman aid in rebuilding the city because of their sense of self-sufficiency. Just so, spiritually, is the Laodicean church. They do not know that they are "wretched, pitiable, poor, blind, and naked" (= anything but self-sufficient, v. 17b).

Since they are so needy, the risen Christ counsels change in threefold form. First, "buy from me gold refined by fire (= purified faith, 1 Pet. 1:6–7) . . . and white garments (= righteous character, 3:4; 4:4; 19:7–8) . . . and salve to anoint your eyes" (so professed Christians, in a city that claimed to be able to treat eye problems, can have clear spiritual vision, v. 18). Second, "those whom I love, I reprove and chasten (Prov. 3:1–12; Heb. 12:5–11); so be zealous and repent" (v. 19). Third, "I stand at the door and knock; if anyone hears my voice and opens the door, I will come in to him and eat with him, and he with me" (v. 21; S. of Sol. 5:2). The reference is not to the parousia, as in James 5:9, because at the parousia the coming of Christ is cosmic in its dimensions (Rev. 19:11–21; Luke 17:22–24). Here Christ's entry is communal at best, possibly individual. His word is addressed to the church or the individual; his entry is into the church or the individual; his eating is with the church or the individual (Luke 24:13–32, 36–43). When this happens is determined not by God's cosmic plan for history as a whole but by the community's or individual's decision to grant entry. In contrast to the Roman power to requisition lodging, the messianic king refuses to force an entry. If admitted, however, he will come in and share supper (= the evening meal at which one sat and talked for a long time with family and friends).

The customary promise precedes the final exhortation. "Those who conquer (= those who do not worship the beast or have his mark on them), I will grant to sit with me on my throne (Rev. 20:4–5; Matt. 19:28), as I myself conquered and sat down with my Father on his throne (Rev. 20:5; Matt. 26:64)" (v. 21).

The recurring exhortation concludes this letter. "Those who have ears, let them hear what the Spirit says to the churches" (v. 22). Each of these letters is a message from the risen Christ (Rev. 2:1, 8, 12, 18; 3:1, 7, 14), given through a prophetic utterance of the Spirit.

Having surveyed the seven letters to the seven churches, it now becomes possible to attempt a description of their situation.

They were subject to external pressures from both pagans (1:9; 2:9; 2:13) and Jews (2:9; 3:9) because they were Christians. This was not state-sponsored oppression but was the type of abuse minorities generally experience at the hands of the majority culture when the former is noticeably different, as in Heb. 10:32–34 and 1 Peter 4:3–4.

They faced internal problems from false teachers (2:2—apostles; 2:6, 15—Nicolaitans; 2:14—those who hold the teaching of Balaam; 2:20–23—the prophetess Jezebel). These various false teachers seem to be variations of the same positions: advocacy of eating food offered to idols and immorality, that is, accommodation to the pagan culture. In other words, some members of the churches actively advocated accommodationism.

The churches faced the perennial problems of spiritual lethargy (2:4—backsliding; 3:4—soiled garments; 3:15—loss of zeal, neither hot nor cold; 1:9; 2:2, 3, 19; 3:10—patient endurance is needed).

This picture of the churches is interesting for what it does not present us. It does not depict the churches as universally poor. Only one church, Smyrna, is so portrayed (2:9). The problem of accommodation was one that applied only to Christians who were reasonably well-to-do. In addition, it does not depict the Christians as totally estranged from the culture. Again, the problem of accommodation points to a desire on the part of Christians to be integrated into the larger economic society. Third, it does not offer us a picture of churches subject to a present, pervasive, state-sponsored persecution. Only one church, Pergamum (2:13), had had a martyr, and only one! Any serious persecution is alluded to as a future event (2:10; 2:22; 3:10). Contrary to the oft-repeated claim that apocalyptic was written by and for deprived, oppressed people who had no political or economic power and were alienated from the larger society, the Revelation to John, like the Shepherd of Hermas, "Visions" 1–4,[5] seems addressed, for the most part, to complacent, spiritually anemic Christians. They seem to be concerned mostly with making an accommodation to the larger pagan society so as to share in its economic prosperity and to avoid the social sanctions of pagans and Jews.[6] The churches are in danger of losing their Christian identity. The issue at stake is that of assimilation to pagan culture. It is a first-commandment issue ("You shall have no other gods beside me," Ex. 20:3). That the church is in danger of losing its identity through corruption by an alien culture is, for early Christians, a sign of the end times (Pastoral Epistles; 2 Peter; 1 Clement; Ascension of Isaiah 3:14–4:22).

The basic issue at this point is how the seven visions that follow (4:1–22:5) relate to the seven letters (2:1–3:22). If the seven letters show the problem confronted by the church on earth to be that of accommodation, consciously or unconsciously, to Roman imperial culture, what roles do the seven visions of the shift of the ages play?

What are the visions about? At the risk of oversimplification, one might say that the first six visions focus primarily on the predicted time of tribulation that the risen Christ has said is coming upon the whole earth (2:10, 22; 3:10), and the seventh vision concentrates mostly on the eschatological vindication and blessings promised by Christ to faithful Christians beyond such suffering (2:7b, 10b, 11b, 17b, 26–28; 3:5, 12, 21).

Why are visions employed by the prophet? The visions that focus on the tribulation attempt to set forth in the starkest terms possible the ultimate incompatibility between Christian values and those of Roman imperial culture. Eventual recognition of this fact by the state, the prophet's visions say, will result in state-sponsored persecution of Christians. Recognition of this incompatibility by Christians will result in their refusal to bear the mark of the beast (= to be assimilated into pagan religiosity), whatever the cost.

The final vision, which concentrates on the last judgment and the eschatological blessings bestowed upon God's faithful people, speaks a word about the destiny of both the persecutor and his allies on the one hand and that of the faithful Christians on the other. In this way the Apocalypse of John links the opening letters to the seven churches (= the church on earth) and the seven visions of the shift of the ages that follow. Recognizing this unity is critical to an accurate reading of Revelation. To the first of these visions of the end times (4:1–8:2) we now turn.

3

THE SEVEN VISIONS OF THE END TIMES (4:1–22:5)

THE SEVEN SEALS
REVELATION 4:1–8:1

After the opening call and commission of the prophet John (1:9–20) and his letters to the seven churches in the province of Asia (2:1–3:22), the Apocalypse presents the reader with seven visions of the shift of the ages: (1) 4:1–8:1; (2) 8:2–11:18; (3) 11:19–13:18; (4) 14:1–20; (5) 15:1–16:21; (6) 17:1–19:5; and (7) 19:6–22:5. These seven visions all present the same basic themes but with variations (recapitulation). Each of the seven visions begins with a scene in heaven that, in some way or another, offers reassurance to the hearers before what may be regarded as "bad news" is forthcoming. The first two visions (4:1–8:1 and 8:2–11:18) focus on the tribulation that precedes the end, especially insofar as it affects Christians. They are organized the same way and in terms of their meaning are virtually synonymous. The first, 4:1–8:1, is a thought unit composed of two parts: 4:1–5:14, an opening scene in heaven, and 6:1–8:1, the opening of the seven seals. To its first part we now turn.

4:1–5:14 = Opening Scene in Heaven

Before portraying the eschatological woes that the risen Christ had predicted would come upon God's people (3:10), the prophet John offers his readers a vision of what he has seen: a vision of the throne (chap. 4) and a vision of the scroll of destiny and the Lamb (chap. 5). The two chapters are organized in similar ways.

Revelation 4 (God)	Revelation 5 (The Lamb)
God's glory (4:2b–8a)	The Lamb's glory (5:5–7)
Worship of God (8b–11)	Worship of the Lamb (8–12)
First hymn (8b)	First hymn (9–10)

Revelation 4 (God) *Revelation 5 (The Lamb)*
Narrative (9–10) Narrative (11–12a)
Second hymn (11) Second hymn (12b)

The opening scene concludes in 5:13–14 with a combined worship of God and the Lamb.

The function of these two chapters is reassure the Christian hearers before they are told about the coming tribulation. They need to know from the start that the God who is in control is gracious and that the tribulation is actually a part of the Lamb's saving activity. Neither meaningless chaos nor merciless fate rules human affairs. The cosmos belongs to God and the Lamb. The dual scene in heaven makes this clear.

Chapter 4 offers a vision of God in heaven. The prophet, who has heard the risen Christ speak like a trumpet in 1:10, 18, now hears him speak again: "Come up hither, and I will show you what must take place after this" (v. 1b). Ancient Jewish and Christian apocalypses are of two types: type one, those with an otherworldly journey (e.g., *Jewish*. 1 Enoch 1–36; 1 Enoch 37–71; T. Levi 2–5; Testament of Abraham; *Christian*. Ascension of Isaiah 6–11; Apocalypse of Paul), and type two, those without such a journey (e.g., *Jewish*. 1 Enoch 85–90; 1 Enoch 93:1–10; 91:11–17; 4 Ezra; 2 Bar.; *Christian*. Apocalypse of Peter; Hermas, "Visions," 1–5). The Apocalypse of John reflects both types (e.g., 1:9–3:22 = type two, a revelation with no heavenly journey; 4:1–8:1 = type one, a revelation involving a heavenly journey). The reference to coming up to heaven in 4:1–2 is to the prophet's heavenly journey as part of his reception of a revelation. It violates the text to read it as a reference to the churches being taken up out of the world before the tribulation.

"In the Spirit" (= prophetic inspiration, v. 2a) John sees "a throne . . . in heaven, with one seated on the throne" (v. 2b; cf 1 Kings 22:19; Isa. 6:1–4; Ezek. 1:26; Dan. 7:9; 1 Enoch 14:18–23; 4QS 1). In what follows, heaven is described as the throne room of an oriental monarch, with the ruler surrounded by his court (vv. 2b–8a). God's appearance is glorious ("like jasper and carnelian"—v. 3) and awesome ("From the throne issue flashes of lightning, and voices and peals of thunder"—v. 5). He[1] is surrounded by twenty-four elders (v. 4), His heavenly council (1 Kings 22:19; Ps. 89:7; Job 1:6; 2:1; Dan. 7:9–10; 1 Enoch 1:4, 9; 47:3–5; 60:2; in LXX Isa. 24:23, members of the heavenly council are called "elders"), and by the four living creatures (v. 6b), the seraphim, a high order of angels (Isa. 6:2; 1 Enoch 71:7; 2 Enoch 20:1; 21:1; 22:2). Before Him are the seven spirits of God (v. 5b), the Holy Spirit (1:4b).

The God who sits on the throne is the object of worship. The cherubim, day and night, never cease to sing: "Holy, holy, holy, is the Lord God Almighty" (v. 8b; cf. Isa. 6:3; 1 Enoch 39:12; 2 Enoch 19:6). The twenty-four elders, falling down before Him, cast their crowns before the throne (= an act of homage; cf. Tacitus, *Annals* 15:29; Cicero, *Pro Sestio* 27; Plutarch, *Lucullus* 522), singing "Worthy art Thou, our Lord and God, to receive glory and honor and power, for Thou didst create all things, and by Thy will they existed and were created" (v. 11). The basis for the praise directed to the one sitting on the throne is that He is creator.

This vision of the throne in heaven is a picture of the awesome power of God. The God of the Apocalypse, however, is not only the one who sits on the throne (power). The throne is surrounded by a rainbow (v. 3b; cf. Gen. 9:12–13; Ezek. 1:28), the promise of mercy. A throne (power) surrounded by a rainbow (mercy)—this is the first thing John shares of what he saw to give reassurance to his readers.

Chapter 5 follows up with a vision of the Book of Destiny and the Lamb. John sees in the right hand of God (= the hand of authority) a scroll (= the book of destiny in which God's will from before the creation is written down; cf. Ps. 139:16; Dan. 10:21; 1 Enoch 81:1–3; 93:1–3; 103:1–3; 106:19–107:1) sealed with seven seals (v. 1; i.e., by a signet ring pressed into the clay or wax, so perfectly sealed by divine authority).

Jewish and early Christian writers had various ways of speaking about God's sovereignty over the world and its affairs. Sometimes the language was that of foreknowledge on God's part (Testament of Moses 12:4–5, 13 speaks of God as the one who has *foreseen* what will happen from the creation to the end of the age).

At other times the image was that of God's having preordained, appointed, allotted, or decreed what should happen in human history (1 Enoch 5:2, "as God has *decreed*, so everything is done"; 1QS 3:16, "when, as *ordained* for them, they come into being, it is in accord with His gracious design"; 4:18, "God has *ordained* an end for falsehood"; 4:25, "until the *determined* end"; 1 QM 17:5, "the day *appointed* by Him for the defeat and overthrow of the Prince of the kingdom of wickedness").

In still other contexts the picture used was that of heavenly books in which God's will has been written down before Creation, which have been sealed by divine authority, and which, when opened, will set in motion God's will on the earth (4 Ezra 6:20, "the *books* shall be opened . . . and all shall see it [the end time] together"). It is the last-mentioned strategy that is employed in Revelation 5. It is not to be taken in a wooden, determineistic way but as a poetic image expressing God's control over human history.

The problem is that there is no one worthy to open the scroll and to break its seals (vv. 3–4), that is, to set in motion God's will upon the earth. The inability to do so was not due to lack of strength but to moral unworthiness.[2] This reduces the prophet to tears. One of the twenty-four elders consoles him: "Weep not; lo, the Lion of the tribe of Judah (Gen. 49:9–10; Testament of Judah 24:5; 4 Ezra 12:31–32), the Root of David (Isa. 11:1) has conquered (= been faithful unto death, 3:21), so that he can open the scroll and its seven seals" (v. 5; for the same idea in slightly different words, see Phil. 2:8–11). Only one who has died rather than sin has the moral authority to set in motion God's will upon the earth.

Who is this Lion who is worthy? John sees near the throne "a Lamb standing, as though it had been slain, with seven horns (= perfect power; Deut. 33:17; 1 Kings 22:11; 1 Enoch 89:46; Testament of Benjamin 3:8) and with seven eyes (= perfect knowledge; Zech. 4:10), which are the seven spirits of God sent out into all the earth" (v. 6). The Lamb with perfect power recalls the conventional Jewish image of horned lambs that destroy Israel's enemies (1 Enoch 90:9; Testament of Joseph 19:8–10; Jerusalem Targum on Ex. 1:15). The image of a Lamb, therefore, does not reflect discontinuity with the image of the Lion. Both are symbols of power. The reference to the Lamb's being slain is a clear reference to Jesus' death. To my knowledge, only in 4 Ezra 7:29–30 does Jewish apocalyptic refer to the Messiah's death. There his death denotes his finitude. (After the 400-year temporary messianic kingdom, "my Son the Messiah shall die, and all who draw human breath. And the world shall be turned back to primeval silence for seven days, as it was at the first beginnings; so that no one shall be left".) He, like all flesh, is mortal. In Rev. 5:5–7, however, Jesus' death is his conquest of sin (vv. 5–7) and the ground for his moral ability to set in motion God's will upon the earth. His power is rooted in his obedience to God. It is this that enables him to ransom people for God (5:9).

When the Lamb takes the scroll (v. 8), heavenly worship focuses on him. The twenty-four elders sing a new song: "Worthy art Thou to take the scroll and to open its seals" (vv. 9–10). When Israel was delivered by Yahweh from Egyptian slavery, the first thing they did when they passed through the sea was to sing a song to the Lord: "Then Moses and the people of Israel sang this song to the Lord, saying, 'I will sing to the Lord, for he has triumphed gloriously; the horse and the rider he has thrown into the sea'"(Ex. 15:1). Thereafter, following a new act of deliverance performed by the Lord on their behalf, Israelites would sing "a new song" (Ps. 40:3; 96:1; 98:1; 144:9; 149:1; Isa. 42:10). A new song celebrates a new deliverance.

So likewise in Rev. 5:9–10. In anticipation of the new and final deliverance that would be performed when God's will is set in motion upon the earth by the Lamb's opening the seven seals of the book of destiny, the heavenly council sings a "new song." The praise reaches beyond just the council of twenty-four. "Many angels, numbering myriads of myriads and thousands of thousands," join in the chorus: "Worthy is the Lamb who was slain to receive power and wealth and wisdom and might and honor and glory and blessing" (v. 12). If in chapter 5 worship was directed to Him who sat upon the throne, here it is addressed to the Lamb.

In early Christianity prayer was addressed to Jesus (22:20b; 1 Cor. 16:22b); Jesus and the Father were believed to act together to answer prayer (1 Thess. 3:11; 2 Thess. 2:16; John 14:13–14); and worship was offered to Jesus (e.g., Matt. 2:2, 11; 14:33; 28:9; 28:17; Ascension of Isaiah 7:17, 21–22; 8:18; 9:31, 36; 10:6; Pliny, *Letters* 10.96, "on an appointed day they had been accustomed to meet before daybreak and to sing a hymn antiphonally to Christ as to a god"). The worship of the Lamb in Revelation 5 fits naturally into the larger context of early Christian piety.[3]

The heavenly worship ends in chapter 5 with worship directed to both God and the Lamb (7:10b; 11:15b; 12:10b–12; 19:6b–8). "And I heard every creature in heaven and on earth and under the earth and in the sea, and all therein, saying, 'To Him who sits upon the throne and to the Lamb be blessing and honor and glory and might for ever and ever'" (v. 13). And the seraphim responded, "Amen!" And the heavenly council fell down and worshiped (v. 14).

Revelation 4–5 offers a lengthy opening scene in heaven to reassure the auditors of the Apocalypse. God the Creator is in control of history. The God who is in control is merciful. The Lamb who conquered (= died rather than be disobedient to God) has thereby the moral authority to open the book of destiny (= set in motion God's will upon the earth). Now that he has taken the scroll from God's right hand, in anticipation of the great deliverance that will ensue, the heavenly hosts join with all creation to sing the praises of God and the Lamb. The contrast between the pitiful plight of the church on earth conveyed by 2:1–3:22 and the awesome majesty of God and the Lamb portrayed in 4:1–5:11 is stark. It is in light of the latter that Christians should hear the words of 6:1–8:1. A merciful God is in control! With this assurance, it is possible to turn to the section dealing with the seven seals.

6:1–8:1 = The Seven Seals

It is important that the reader recognize that what follows is due to the Lamb's initiative and falls within the scope of God's will. There are seven seals that are opened by the Lamb, with an interlude between the sixth and the seventh (7:1–17). The first four belong together. The image of the four horsemen (Zech. 1:7–15; 6:1–8) functions in Revelation as a symbol of the tribulation.

The opening of the first seal, 6:1–2.

Out came a white horse whose rider had a bow. This echo of the dreaded Parthian warriors who had, on more than one occasion, defeated the Roman armies is used to symbolize wars of conquest.

The opening of the second seal, 6:3–4.

Out came a bright red horse whose rider was a catalyst for people's slaying one another. This symbolizes internal anarchy among nations.

The opening of the third seal, 6:5–6.

Out came a black horse whose rider had a balance in his hand (= a scales). An audition confirms the meaning of the vision: "A quart of wheat (= the amount required for a man for food for one day) for a denarius (= a day's wage), and three quarts of barley (= a low-grade subsistence for a family for one day) for a denarius, but do not harm oil and wine." It would take all a worker could earn in a day just to feed himself adequately; to provide for his family also could be done only at a subsistence level. This horse and rider, then, symbolize famine.

The opening of the fourth seal, 6:7–8.

Out came a pale horse whose rider's name was "Death." Hades (= the realm of the dead; 20:14) followed him. The two were given power over a fourth of the earth, "to kill with sword and with famine and with pestilence and by wild beasts of the earth." This is clearly death.

The four horsemen, then, are conquest, anarchy, famine, and death. They symbolize the great tribulation of Jewish and Christian expectation.[4]

Jewish. Since Jewish apocalyptic eschatology was extremely diverse in its details, one cannot expect to find a homogeneous system of teaching within it. Every theme has its variations. Nevertheless, certain constants can be found. One theme is that there is to be a period of intense suffering immediately preceding the end: the woes of the Messiah, the birth pangs of the New Age, the tribulation, the time of distress, or simply judgment.

For some Jewish sources, the tribulation was past already (Jub. 23:11–25); for some it was present (Dan. 12:1; Assumption of Moses 8–9); for others it was future (2 Bar. 25–29; 1 QM).

For some it will be God's people who will suffer (Dan. 7:21–22; 12:1; Assumption of Moses 8–9; 1 QM 1:11–12); for others it will be the Gentiles (Apocalypse of Abraham 29–30; 1 Enoch 99–100); for still others it will touch both (2 Bar. 29:1–2; 48:31–32), with God's people protected during it (2 Bar. 29:2; 71:1).

The length of the tribulation varied (a week = seven years, Dan. 12:1; 40 years, 1 QM; 12 periods, 2 Bar. 27), if it was a concern at all.

For some authors the tribulation was of primary concern (2 Bar. 25–29; 1 Enoch 91–105; Sibylline Oracles 3; 4 Ezra); for others it was of marginal interest (Adam and Eve 29:7; Testament of Dan 6:6; Testament of Levi 4:1); while for others it held no interest at all (1 Enoch 1–36; 1 Enoch 38–44, 58–71; Psalms of Solomon; 2 Enoch).

The functions of the tribulation also varied. When it is upon Israel, it is understood as a test and/or as a means to bring her back to God (Jub. 23:16, 26, 27–29; Deut. 4:30). When it is upon Gentiles, it is understood as an attempt to gain repentance (Sibylline Oracles 3; 1 Enoch 50:2–5) or as punishment within history (Apocalypse of Abraham 30). Sometimes it is called "judgment" and is believed to fall upon all (2 Bar. 48:31–32).

Early Christian. The notion of a period of intense suffering preceding the shift of the ages carried over into early Christian belief. Again there is diversity of opinion.

For some it was present (1 Cor. 7:26; 1 Pet. 4:12–19; Eusebius, *Church History* 6.6, of one Jude at the beginning of the third century); for others it was future (Mark 13//Matt. 24; Hermas, "Visions," 1–4; Didache 16:5).

Most assumed that God's people would suffer (Mark 13//Matt. 24; Hermas, "Visions," 1–4; Epistle of Barnabas 4:9–14; Didache 16:5; Justin, *Trypho* 110; Irenaeus, *Against Heresies* 5.26.1; Apocalypse of Peter 2; Hippolytus, *Treatise of Christ and Antichrist* 10, 60). For some it would include both Christians and non-Christians (1 Peter 4:12–19).

The length of the tribulation was of little concern, except that some believed God in His mercy would shorten the period (Mark 13:20//Matt. 24:22).

For some the period of suffering was of prime importance (Hermas, "Visions," 1–4); for others it was integral but not central (Mark 13//Matt. 24; Paul); for others it was of no concern (Fourth Gospel; Hebrews).

Its function was primarily in the interest of Christian watchfulness: Be alert so as not to fall away (Mark 13; Didache 16; Hermas, "Visions," 1–4). As regards non-Christians, it had the quality of judgment but held the hope of repentance (1 Peter 4:17–18).

Revelation. When Revelation is read in light of this aspect of apocalyptic thinking, one finds interesting correlations.

The tribulation is in the imminent future (2:10; 3:10). It comes before the parousia (6:1–8 is before 6:12–17; 8:7–9:21 is before 11:15–18; 17:1–6 is before 19:1–10). It will come upon both God's people (2:10; 22–25; 3:10; 6:9–11; 7:1–8, 14; 8:3–4; 12:17; 14:12–13; 16:15; 17:6; 18:4) and the Gen-

tiles (chap. 14; chaps. 15, 16). God's people will be accorded spiritual protection during the distress (7:1–8; 11:1–2). Its length is of finite duration
(2:10; 10 days = a symbolic number). It is a central concern of the Apocalypse (six of the seven visions focus on it). It functions for Christians as a
test (3:10, 19) and as a motivation for faithfulness. For non-Christians it
functions as an opportunity to repent, an opportunity that is not taken
advantage of (9:20–21; 16:9, 11, 21).

The opening of the fifth seal,[5] 6:9–11.

John now sees under the heavenly altar "the souls of those who had
been slain for the word of God and for the witness they had borne" (v. 9;
cf. b. Shabbat 152b, "the souls of the righteous are kept under the throne
of glory"). Assumed here is what has been called the intermediate state (=
a state of conscious existence between the death of an individual and the
resurrection of the body at the final consummation). One finds a developed
concept of the intermediate state in some circles of postbiblical Judaism
(1 Enoch 22:8–13; 4 Ezra 7). This state is assumed in New Testament
sources like Luke 16:19–30; 23:43; Phil. 1:21–23; 2 Cor. 5:8 and in non-
canonical apocalypses like the Ascension of Isaiah 9 and the Apocalypse of
Paul 14, 16. One also finds it assumed in the Revelation to John here in
6:9–11 and elsewhere in 7:14–17 and 14:13. In all these sources, the intermediate state is not a probationary period but is one in which judgment is
a present as well as a future reality.[6]

These martyrs cried out for divine vindication: "How long before
Thou wilt judge and avenge our blood on those who dwell upon the
earth?" (v. 10; cf. Ps. 79:10; Hab. 1:2; Testament of Moses 10:10; 1 Enoch
47:2–4; Ascension of Isaiah 9:6–8; Luke 18:1–8). This paragraph shows
that the tribulation (= the four horsemen) will include the martyrdom of
Christians. In response to their cry for vindication "they were each given
a white robe (= a reflection of their spiritual purity, 3:4) and told to rest a
little longer, until the number of their brethren should be complete, who
were to be killed as they themselves had been" (v. 11). It was characteristic
of apocalyptic thought to assume that God had foreordained a certain
number of martyrdoms that must be accomplished before He would intervene to bring an end to the present evil age (1 Enoch 47:1–4; 2 Bar. 23:5;
4 Ezra 4:33–43). This again is a reflection of the belief that history, even
down to its details, is under the control of God.

The opening of the sixth seal, 6:12–17.

Human suffering is followed by conventional cosmic disturbances expected just prior to the day of the Lord: earthquakes occur (Amos 8:8; 9:5;
4 Ezra 5:8; 9:3); the sun is darkened and the moon becomes like blood

(Joel 2:31; Testament of Moses 10:5; Mark 13:24); the stars fall like figs from a tree shaken by the wind (Isa. 34:4; Testament of Moses 10:5; Mark 13:25); the sky vanishes like a scroll that is rolled up (Isa. 34:4); and mountains and islands are removed from their places (Testament of Moses 10:4). In the face of imminent judgment the inhabitants of the earth hide in the caves and among the rocks of the mountains (Isa. 2:10) and call on the mountains and the rocks to hide them from God's face (Hos. 10:8): "For the great day of their (= God and the Lamb) wrath has come, and who can stand before it?" (v. 17; cf. 1 Enoch 62:3–5).

John's vision of the great tribulation just prior to the end of the ages reflects a conventional Jewish and Christian agenda of events.

Jewish. The Jewish Apocalypse of Abraham 29–30 says that God will send ten plagues before the age of justice. They include these: sorrow from much need; fiery conflagration for the cities; destruction by pestilence among cattle; famine; earthquake and sword; hail and snow; wild beasts; pestilence and hunger; execution by sword and flight in distress; and thunder, voices, earthquakes. Only then does God say: "I will sound the trumpet out of the air, and I will send my Chosen One" (31). In the Jewish apocalypse, 2 Baruch 26–27, the agenda for the tribulation is similar. Present there also are death, sword, famine, earthquake, demons, fire from heaven, havoc and oppression, wickedness and impurity, and chaos.

Christian. The catastrophes preceding the end in Revelation 6 are similar to those found in the Synoptic apocalypse (Mark 13//Luke 21// Matt. 24). The following chart makes this clear.

Revelation 6	Mark 13	Luke 21	Matthew 24
1. Conquest (1–2)	wars (7–8)	wars (9–10)	wars (6–7)
2. Anarchy (3–4)	—	tumults (9)	—
3. Famine (5–6)	famines (8b)	famine (11)	famine (7)
4. Death/pestilence (7–8)	—	pestilence (11)	—
5. Cry for vindication (9–11)	—	—	—
6. Earthquake (12)	earthquakes (8b)	earthquakes (11)	earthquakes (7)
7. Sun darkened (12)	sun dark (24)	sun dark (25)	sun dark (29)
8. Moon as blood (12)	moon/blood (24)	moon/blood (25)	moon/blood (29)

Revelation 6	*Mark 13*	*Luke 21*	*Matthew 24*
9. Stars fall (13)	stars fall (24)	stars fall (25)	stars fall (29)
10. Sky vanishes (14)	—	—	—
11. Mountains moved (14)	—	—	—
12. People afraid (15–17)	—	fear (26)	—

Of the three versions of the Synoptic apocalypse, Luke 21 is closest to Rev. 6:1–17. Such comparisons show beyond any doubt that the depiction of the tribulation in Rev. 6:1–17 employs a conventional agenda. One of the distinctives of the portrayal in Revelation 6 is the focus on the martyrdoms of Christians and their cries for vindication. This makes it unmistakable that for the prophet John the tribulation will involve Christian martyrdoms. Since Christians will suffer during the tribulation, what can enable them to endure? It is to this issue that the interlude of 7:1–17 is addressed.

The interlude, 7:1–17.

The interlude consists of two scenes: one of the church on earth (vv. 1–8), the other of the church in heaven (vv. 9–17).

The first scene involves the sealing of the servants of God on earth (7:1–8). The prophet sees four angels holding back the four winds of the earth (= divine retribution, Jer. 4:11–12; 18:17; Ezek. 5:2; 12:14; Isa. 41:16; 1 Enoch 7:6; 34:3; 60:11–21). They are commanded by yet another angel: "Do not harm the earth or the sea or the trees, till we have sealed the servants of God upon their foreheads," as spiritual protection (v. 3; Ezek. 9). Faithful servants of God will be "preserved through (not from!) the great persecution that is about to be unleashed upon them like a mighty devastating wind."[7]

These servants of God are described as the 144,000 (v. 4), 12,000 from each of the twelve tribes of Israel (vv. 5–8).[8] The list of tribes offered here is problematic. Both Manasseh and Joseph are included, although the former is included in the latter, while Dan is excluded. Dan is likely omitted because of the tribe's bad associations. The tribe was early associated with idolatry (Judg. 18:30); later it was the site of one of the two great shrines in the Northern Kingdom (1 Kings 12:29). In the Testament of Dan 5:6, Satan is said to be the prince (= guardian angel) of the tribe. Irenaeus, *Against Heresies* 5.30.2, said the Antichrist would come from Dan. Symbolizing all that the prophet John regarded as negative, Dan is dropped from his list of God's faithful, and another, more appropriate, tribe is split into two to ensure the necessary twelve.

Who are these one hundred forty-four thousand? In this context in the Apocalypse they are the full number of faithful believers alive when the events, the tribulation, take place.[9] They are the spiritual Israel, the church (Acts 15:14–18; Rom. 11:17–24; Gal. 6:16; Phil. 3:3; James 1:1; 1 Peter 1:1; 2:9). The point of the sealing is protection for God's people (= faithful Christians) during the tribulation so they will not apostatize. The conviction that God protects His people during the messianic woes was characteristic of Jewish apocalypses. For example, 2 Bar. 29:2 and 71:1 speak about protection for God's people during the great period of trial preceding the end.

The second scene in the interlude comes in Rev. 7:9–17. It consists of two parts: a heavenly celebration (7:9–12) and a heavenly explanation (7:13–17).

The heavenly celebration (vv. 9–12) involves a "great multitude which no man could number, from every nation, from all tribes and peoples and tongues (= the universality of the church, Gen. 15:5), standing before the throne and before the Lamb, clothed in white robes (= the garments of heaven; 3:5; 4:4), with palm branches (= signs of victory, 2 Macc. 10:7; 1 Macc. 13:51; Testament of Naphtali 5:4) in their hands" (v. 9). As 7:14 will show, the great multitude is the same group as the one hundred forty-four thousand. In 7:1–8 the church militant was the focus; in 7:9–17 the reference is to the church triumphant. In both cases, it is the church to which the language refers.

Now in heaven the church triumphant joins with the heavenly hosts in their worship of God. The church cries: "Salvation belongs to our God who sits on the throne, and to the Lamb!" (v. 10). The angels, the elders, and the cherubim around the throne reply Amen, and then proceed with their own worship: "Blessing and glory and wisdom and thanksgiving and honor and power and might be to our God for ever and ever! Amen" (vv. 11–12).

The heavenly explanation comes in 7:13–17. One of the twenty-four elders asks the seer, "Who are these, clothed in white robes, and whence have they come?" (v. 13). He answers his own question forthwith: "These are they who have come out of the great tribulation (referred to in 6:1–17); they have washed their robes (= prepared themselves to be in the divine presence, Ex. 19:10, 14) and made them white in the blood of the Lamb" (v. 14).

It is because the church militant has endured through their sufferings that they stand in the presence of God in glory. "*Therefore* are they before the throne of God" (v. 15). To them belong the blessings of heaven: "They shall hunger no more, neither thirst any more (v. 16; 21:6; 22:2) . . . and God will wipe away every tear from their eyes" (v. 17; 21:4). They have endured because they were sealed by divine order (7:3). The point is clear. Christian faithfulness, while a human act, is enabled by divine grace.

The opening of the seventh seal, 8:1.

"When the Lamb opened the seventh seal. . . . " Our expectations are enormous. What are the glories of heaven to follow the agonies of the great tribulation? John's answer at this point is this: "There was silence in heaven for about half an hour" (8:1). Explanation of this statement requires two levels of comment—one theological, the other literary or rhetorical. Theologically, the seer refers to the cosmic silence, the return of the cosmos to its original state, prior to the new creation (4 Ezra 7:30, "And the world shall be turned back to primeval silence for seven days, as it was at the first beginnings; so that no one shall be left"). Rhetorically, we are dealing with a suspended answer. The story cannot continue once it has arrived at its final resolution. So delay is a strategy to stimulate the hearers' interest without arriving at an untimely end. After all, there are six more visions yet to come. At this point a dramatic pause is in order.

The first vision has ended. Its overall message is clearcut. The God who is in control of the world is merciful (chap. 4). The sinless Lamb sets in motion God's will upon the earth (chap. 5). Although the shift of the ages involves suffering (chap. 6), God protects His people through the tribulation so that they persevere into the New Age (chap. 7). Having reached this point, the reader is ready for the second vision (8:2–11:18). To that we now turn.

THE SEVEN TRUMPETS
REVELATION 8:2–11:18

After the opening letters to the seven churches (2:1–3:22) there are seven visions (4:1–22:5) that cover basically the same events, the shift of the ages. The first two (4:1–8:1 and 8:2–11:18) are very similar, not only in arrangement but also in meaning. Both begin with a scene in heaven that functions to offer reassurance to the auditors before the seven-part vision of the events of the end time is given. Both cycles focus on the significance of the tribulation for Christians. In both cycles, there is an interlude between the sixth and the seventh parts of the vision that promises God's protection for His people during the tribulation. Whereas in 4:1–8:1 the vision of the events of the end times was given in terms of the Lamb's opening of seven seals, in 8:2–11:18 it is depicted in terms of the blowing of seven trumpets by seven angels. We have repetition with variation. Attention must now be directed to Cycle Two, 8:2–11:18.

This is a thought unit composed of two parts: 8:2–6, an opening scene in heaven, and 8:7–11:18, the sounding of the seven trumpets.

8:2–6 = Opening Scene in Heaven

All seven visions of the end time in Revelation 4:1–22:5 begin with a scene in heaven that functions to give reassurance to the readers of the Apocalypse. In Cycle Two, 8:2–11:18, this comes in 8:2–6. The unit is arranged in an ABB'A' pattern.

A v. 2 Seven angels are given trumpets.
   B vv. 3–4 An angel lifts the prayers of the saints before God.
   B' v. 5 The angel throws fire upon the earth.
A' v. 6 The seven angels get ready to blow the trumpets.

In part A (v. 2), the seven archangels (Tobit 12:15; 1 Enoch 20:7; 90:21–22) are given seven trumpets. Blowing them will signal the onset of the events of the end time (Isa. 27:13; Joel 2:1; Zeph. 1:16; Psalms of Solomon 11:1; 4 Ezra 6:23; Apocalypse of Zephaniah 9–12; 1 Cor. 15:52; 1 Thess. 4:16; Matt. 24:31).

In part B (vv. 3–4), another angel comes to the heavenly altar and mingles incense with the prayers of the saints (to make them pleasing to God). Here, as in Rev. 6:9, an altar stands in heaven (cf. 6:9; 9:13; 14:18; 16:7). Heavenly worship is conducted in relation to the altar. This can be understood only against the backdrop of beliefs about heavenly worship in Jewish and Christian apocalyptic writings.[10]

Jewish. In Jewish apocalyptic writings, heavenly worship takes place in either a heavenly temple (1 Enoch 14:10–20; Testament of Levi 5:1) or a throne room (1 Enoch 60:2; 61:8; Testament of Moses 10:3). Usually the two are combined (1 Enoch 14:10–20; Testament of Levi 5:1; Testament of Moses 10:3). Every scene of heavenly worship directs all praise to the only God (Testament of Levi 3:5, 8; Testament of Abraham 14:8).

The participants in this worship are all the inhabitants of heaven. This includes angels (1 Enoch 47:22; 60:1; 78:1, 8), the righteous dead (1 Enoch 39:4–7; 60:2), and sometimes the visionary while on his heavenly journey (1 Enoch 39:9; 71:11–12; Testament of Abraham 14:6–8, 16; 20:18). Some angels have a priestly role in which they are responsible for the worship (1 Enoch 71:1; Testament of Levi 3:5–6). Others, "those who do not sleep" (1 Enoch 14:23; 39:12–13; 47:2; 71:7), give praise to God day and night.

Worship of God is primarily praise (1 Enoch 39:7, 9, 12; 40:3; 41:7; 47:2; 61:7; Testament of Levi 3:8; Testament of Abraham 14:11; 20:17–18).

It also consists of angelic intercessory prayer (1 Enoch 39:5; 40:6; Testament of Abraham 14:6–10).

There is often a link between earth and heaven involved in this heavenly worship. Sometimes the prayers of the righteous on earth are brought before God in heaven by angels with the result that judgment follows (Tobit 12:15; 1 Enoch 9, 10, 47, 97, 99, 104). At other times the angels during worship remember the saints on earth (1 Enoch 39:5; 40:6; Testament of Abraham 14:6).

Heavenly worship functions in Jewish apocalypses to portray God as in control of history and to show what the blessed future of the righteous will be like. This serves as a stimulus to proper conduct by the readers.

Christian. In Christian apocalypses heaven is described predominantly as a temple (Ascension of Isaiah 10:6). The area in which worship occurs is one where there is an altar (Apocalypse of Paul 29; 44). The image of the throne is also found, however (Apocalypse of Paul 44).

The objects of worship in Christian apocalypses are God (Ascension of Isaiah 7:17; 8:18, 22; Apocalypse of Paul 7, 8, 10, 14, 18, 29), Jesus Christ, and the Holy Spirit (Ascension of Isaiah 8:18; 9:27–36). Worship of angels is prohibited (Ascension of Isaiah 7:20–21; 8:4–5).

The worship scenes of Christian apocalypses include the same participants as in the Jewish apocalypses: angels (Ascension of Isaiah 7:14–16; 8:17; 9:29, 42; Apocalypse of Paul 7–10, 14), including the twenty-four elders and four beasts (Apocalypse of Paul 14, 44), the righteous dead (Ascension of Isaiah 9:28, 33, 41; 11:32; Apocalypse of Paul 29, 48), and the seer (Ascension of Isaiah 8:3, 17, 22; 9:31, 33; 10:19).

Worship is most often praise of God (Ascension of Isaiah 7:15–37; 8:3, 13; 9:29–41; Apocalypse of Paul 8, 29, 30) in an unceasing manner (Apocalypse of Paul 10, as one set of angels retires, another group comes into the meeting to worship). Intercessory prayer is also a component as angels go before God on behalf of humans (Apocalypse of Paul 7).

There are links between earthly and heavenly worship. The Apocalypse of Paul 49 says that each of the saints has his own angel who helps him and sings a hymn. In Christian apocalypses heavenly worship functions not only to stimulate proper conduct by its vision of God and the ultimate destiny of the saints but also to affirm the deity of Christ over against the creaturely nature of angels.

Revelation. John uses both images of heaven in the Apocalypse: throne room (Rev. 4; cf. 7:9, 11, 15; 8:3; 14:3; 20:11) and temple (Rev. 7:15; 11:19; 15:5–6, 8; 16:1). In 6:9 and 8:3–5 mention is made of the heavenly altar.

God (Rev. 4; 8:4; 11:16; 15:1–8; 19:5) and Christ (Rev. 5) are objects of worship. Angels are not to be worshiped (Rev. 19:9–10; 22:8–9).

Participants in heavenly worship are angels (5:11; 8:2; 15:1, 6; 19:1), including the twenty-four elders (4:10; 5:8, 14; 19:4) and the four winged creatures who never sleep (4:8–9; 5:8, 11, 14; 15:7; 19:4), and the righteous dead (7:10; 14:1, 3–5; 15:2). Unlike many apocalypses, the seer, John, does not participate in heavenly worship.

Again praise is the standard component of heavenly worship (5:9–10; 15:3–4; 14:8; 19:1–10). Intercessory prayer is also an ingredient in the worship of heaven (5:8; 8:3–6).

Angels offer the prayers of the saints before God (4:8; 8:3–6). These prayers play a role in bringing about the beginning of the events of the end time (8:3–5).

In Revelation heavenly worship serves not only to stimulate proper conduct and affirm Christ's deity but also to reassure Christians that the prayers of the saints make a difference in the working out of God's will upon the earth. Eschatological events follow from worship scenes (chaps. 4–5 are followed by 6:1–8:1; 8:3–5 is followed by 8:7–11:18; 15:2–8 is followed by 16:1–21).[11]

Returning to the scene in heaven in part B' (v. 5), the angel involved in priestly service at the altar, having raised the prayers of the saints to the throne (vv. 3–4), fills the censer (= bowl for incense) with fire from the altar and throws it upon the earth. The purpose of the fire from the altar is the purification of the earth's inhabitants (cf. Isa. 6:1–7 where one of the seraphim takes a coal from the altar and touches Isaiah's lips, saying, "Behold, this has touched your lips; your guilt is taken away, and your sin forgiven").

In part A' (v. 6), the seven angels make ready to blow the seven trumpets. In this paragraph (8:2–6), parts B' (v. 5) and A' (v. 6) are to be considered results of the prayers of the saints in vv. 3–4. When the saints pray, God listens. Christians' prayers make a difference. From the point of view of the prophet John, if saints want to make an ultimate difference in the world, the most important thing they can do is to worship, joining their earthly praise and intercession with the whole company of heaven. The praise component of worship (Rev. 4–5) results in a true vision of how things really are as opposed to how they seem to be (cf. Ps. 73:17). The intercessory component of worship (8:3) is a catalyst for the setting in motion of God's will upon the earth (1 Enoch 9:1–4a, 10–11; 10:1–3—cries for vengeance, mediated by angels, serve to occasion the divine intervention; 1 Enoch 47:1–4—prayers carried to God by angels produce judgment; 1 Enoch 97:5—prayer reaches the Lord and judgment results; cf. Matt. 6:9–13; Luke 18:1–8; 1 Cor. 16:22b; Rev. 22:20b). It is this conviction that finds expression in 8:2–6. After the angel lifts the saints' prayers to God (vv. 3–4), the series of eschatological events begins (8:5–11:18). That the prayers of Christians make a difference is reassurance to believers who will have to endure the tribulation.

8:7–11:18 = The Seven Trumpets

The seven trumpets are basically a recapitulation of the seven seals of 6:1–8:1, that is, repetition with variation.

The first trumpet is sounded, 8:7.

Hail and fire, mixed with blood, fall upon the earth. This sounds very much like the seventh plague of Ex. 9:23–24: "The Lord sent thunder and hail, and fire ran down to the earth. . . . there was hail, and fire flashing continually in the midst of the hail." As in Ex. 9:25, the hail and fire produce devastation upon the earth. "A third of the earth was burnt up, and a third of the trees . . . , and all green grass" (Rev. 8:7). It also echoes beliefs about fire associated with future judgment (Isa. 5:24–25; Jer. 4:4; 21:12; Ezek. 5:2 in context; Amos 1:4, 10, 12, 14; 2:2, 5).

The second trumpet is sounded, 8:8–9.

A third of the sea becomes blood. This sounds very much like the first plague in Ex. 7:20: "All the water . . . turned to blood." As in Ex. 7:21, the fish die, at least a third of them (Rev. 8:9). It also sounds like Zephaniah's oracle of future judgment: "I will sweep away . . . the fish of the sea" (1:3).

The third trumpet is sounded, 8:10–11.

A third of the waters become wormwood and people die because of the water. This has no parallel among the plagues upon Egypt at the Exodus. It rather echoes an oracle in Jeremiah 9:13–18: The Lord says, "Because they have forsaken my law . . . and have not obeyed my voice . . . but have stubbornly followed their own hearts. . . . Behold I will feed this people with wormwood and give them poisonous water to drink." Poisonous water is a punishment for sin. In 4 Ezra 5:9 it is also one of the signs of the end times.

The fourth trumpet is sounded, 8:12–13.

A third of the sun, a third of the moon, and a third of the stars are struck so that a third of their light is darkened. This darkness echoes the ninth plague in Ex. 10:21: "Then the Lord said to Moses, 'Stretch out your hand toward heaven that there may be darkness over the land of Egypt.'" It also is a sign of the last day (Joel 2:2; 2:31; Amos 5:18).

Just as the first four seals (= the four horsemen) in Cycle One were a unit (6:1–8), so are the first four trumpets in Cycle Two. This is made clear by v. 13. An eagle cries with a loud voice: "Woe, woe, woe to those who dwell on the earth, at the blasts of the other trumpets which the three angels are about to blow." Rhetorically this announcement breaks the narrative progression, as it introduces the agonies yet to come.

The fifth trumpet is sounded, 9:1–11 (12).

John sees a star fallen from heaven to earth (= an angel descends from heaven to earth, 1 Enoch 86:1, 3; 88:1). This angel is given the key to the bottomless pit (11:7; 17:8; 20:1–3; 1 Enoch 18:12–16; 19:1–2; 21:1–10). When he opens the shaft to the abyss, out come smoke and locusts with the power of scorpions (= to inflict pain). The locusts are told what they can ravage and for how long. Whereas real locusts harm vegetation but not humans, these angels of judgment (1 Enoch 66:1; 2 Enoch 10:3; Testament of Levi 3:3) are not to harm vegetation but only humans "who have not the seal of God upon their foreheads" (v. 4; cf. 7:3; 22:4). Just as they were with the plagues at the exodus, God's faithful people are exempted from this torment (Ex. 8:22; 9:4, 26; 10:23; 11:7). The locusts are allowed to torture these humans for five months (= the life cycle of locusts) but not to kill them (vv. 5–6). Their appearance is horrible (vv. 7–10; cf. Joel 1:4 and 2:7–10). Their leader is the Destroyer (v. 11). Whereas the first four trumpets unleashed physical torment, the fifth trumpet's effects are what we might call psychic pain. Can anything be worse than the inner agonies that make one wish to die? Two more woes, however, are yet to come (v. 12).

The sixth trumpet is sounded, 9:13–21.

A voice from the altar before God commands the sixth angel to "Release the four angels who are bound at the great river Euphrates" (v. 13). These four come at the head of a great army. The cavalry is twice ten thousand times ten thousand (v. 16). Their appearance is terrible (v. 17); their effect is the death of a third of humankind (vv. 15, 18–19).

After all these events (8:7–9:19) "the rest of mankind, who were not killed by these plagues, did not repent of the works of their hands nor give up worshiping demons and idols of gold and silver and bronze and stone and wood, which cannot either see or hear or walk; nor did they repent of their murders or their sorceries or their immorality or their thefts" (vv. 20–21). The vision has already indicated in at least two ways that the events unleashed by the trumpet blasts were intended to be redemptive. First, the fire thrown on the earth from the heavenly altar aimed to purify humankind (v. 5; remember Isa. 6:1–7). Second, the horrible effects of the tribulation are limited. Only a third of this or that is affected (8:7, 9, 11, 12; 9:15). This is a way of saying that the judgment involved in the tribulation is limited (cf. a similar motif in Mark 13:20, where the time is short-ened). So far in this vision, the tribulation has come upon unbelievers only in an attempt to elicit repentance.

In antiquity one way of viewing human suffering was as divine educa-tion of the sufferer.[12] In its Jewish form, the assumption was usually that the sufferer had strayed, either consciously or unconsciously, from the right path. The pain experienced was the discipline necessary to correct the misdirection (Prov. 3:11–12; Psalms of Solomon 10:1–2; 16:11—"If I sin, discipline me that I may return"; Sirach 18:13; 2 Macc. 6:12). In its Greco-Roman form, the assumption was usually that suffering was not so much correction of misdirection as conditioning that builds one up for greater virtue (Epictetus, *Discourses* l.xxiv.1–3: "'When a difficulty befalls, remember that God, like a physical trainer, has matched you with a rugged young man.' 'What for?' someone says. 'So that you may become an Olympic victor; but that cannot be done without sweat.'"). In early Chris-tian writings both views of suffering as divine education are found, some-times in the same author. Take Paul as an example. On the one hand, Rom. 5:3–4 is very close to the Greco-Roman view: "We rejoice in our suffer-ings, knowing that suffering produces endurance, and endurance produces character, and character produces hope." On the other hand, 1 Cor. 11:29–32 seems to reflect the Jewish background: "But when we are judged by the Lord, we are being chastened so that we may not be condemned along with the world" (v. 32). In the former, suffering develops character; in the latter, it corrects misdirection.

Revelation 3:19 clearly stands within the normal Jewish framework for understanding suffering as educational. The risen Christ says to the Laodiceans: "Those whom I love, I reprove and chasten; so be zealous and repent." It is this view of suffering that underlies Revelation's understand-ing of the function of the tribulation. It has a redemptive intent. In spite of the redemptive divine intent, however, the sufferings of the tribulation do not produce repentance in humans who survive but have not been marked with the seal of God on their foreheads (9:4; 14:1; 22:4).

The interlude, 10:1–11:14.

An interlude comes between the sixth and seventh trumpets, just as an interlude came between the sixth and seventh seals (7:1–17) in Cycle One (4:1–8:1). The interlude consists of four scenes: (1) 10:1–7, a proclamation of the nearness of the end; (2) 10:8–11, the eating of the little scroll; (3) 11:1–2, the measuring of the temple of God; and (4) 11:3–14, the ap-pearance of the two witnesses. Each must be examined in order.

In scene one, 10:1–7, John sees another angel coming down from heaven, "wrapped in a cloud (= the presence of God, Dan. 7:13; Mark

14:62; Acts 1:9), with a rainbow over his head (= a promise of mercy, Gen. 9:13–17; Rev. 4:3), and his face was like the sun (brilliant, 1:16), and his legs like pillars of fire (= another sign of God's presence, Ex. 13:21–22). The angel performs two functions: He brings the little scroll that will play a key role in the next scene (10:8–11) and he makes a proclamation (10:5–7). It is the latter that is central to scene one. This angel sets his right foot on the sea and his left foot on the land (v. 2, that is, his message will be universal in scope) and lifts his right hand to heaven (v. 5, the gesture of taking an oath—Gen. 14:22–23; Deut. 32:40; Dan. 12:7— that is, his message will be truthful). The content of the angel's proclamation is that "there should be no more delay" (v. 6). The universal, truthful proclamation from heaven is that the end is imminent (1:1, 3; 22:7, 12, 20).

In scene two (10:8–11), a voice from heaven commands John to take the scroll from the angel (v. 8). The angel tells the seer to "take it and eat; it will be bitter to your stomach, but sweet as honey in your mouth" (v. 9). The echoes are of Ezek. 2:8–3:3 where the prophet is given a scroll to eat, which in his mouth is sweet as honey (cf. Jer. 15:16–17). This scene is another call scene (remember 1:9–20). It functions to authenticate the prophet's words that follow. Eating a divine book fills the seer with prophetic revelation. If scene one established the nearness of the end, scene two serves to legitimate the message of the prophet John.

In scene three (11:1–2) the prophet is given a measuring rod and is told: "Rise up and measure the temple of God and the altar and those that worship there, but do not measure the court outside the temple; leave that out, for it is given over to the nations, and they will trample over the holy city for forty-two months."[13] Measuring in this context is an act of protection and preservation, as in Zech. 2:1–2, where Jerusalem's being measured is a sign of its protection, and in Ezek. 40–41, where the temple's being measured is a promise of its preservation.

But to what does the temple refer? First, the term used for temple is *naos*, not *hieron*. Whereas the LXX uses *hieron* to refer to the Jerusalem temple generally, it uses *naos* for the most sacred parts of the temple, either the Holy Place (1 Kings 6:17; 2 Chron. 4:22; Ezek. 8:16), or the porch or vestibule (1 Chron. 28:11; 2 Chron. 8:12), or the Holy of Holies (Ps. 28:2). Paul also uses *naos* for the inner portions of the temple (1 Cor. 3:16; 2 Cor. 6:16). In Revelation also the reference to the temple (*naos*) is to the innermost parts, where God's presence dwells in a special way. Second, temple here is used symbolically of the true people of God (1 Cor. 3:16; 2 Cor. 6:16; Eph. 2:19–22; 1 Peter 2:5), the faithful church (= people who have not soiled their garments, 3:4).

To what do the courts outside the *naos*/inner sanctuary refer? It cannot be a reference to the nations (= non-Christians) for they will trample the outer courts (v. 2). This leaves Christians who are not faithful (cf. 2:5; 2:14–16; 2:20–23; 3:2–3). It is they whom the risen Christ reproves and chastens (3:19). Faithless Christians will experience the pains of the tribulation, but their intent is redemptive. This experience of suffering lasts for forty-two months (= a limited time, Dan. 7:25; 12:7). Those who are faithful he protects during the hour of trial that is coming upon the whole earth (3:10; symbolized by the measuring of the inner parts of the temple).

All Christians experience the great tribulation, but its meaning for them differs depending upon whether they are faithful or faithless. The faithless experience the hour of trial as the suffering of discipline to cause them to repent; the faithful experience the pain, but are protected by God from apostasy. In the one case, Christians are off track, and the suffering aims to correct their misdirection. In the case of the other, Christians are on track, and the suffering cannot get them off track because of God's protection. The measuring of the temple's innermost parts symbolizes this protection of the faithful from apostasy. The interlude (10:1–11:13) has so far made three points: The end is near (10:1–7); the prophet John has a divine message (10:8–11); and faithful Christians will be protected from apostasy during the tribulation (11:1–2).

In scene four of the interlude (11:3–13) John is told about the appearing of the two witnesses. "I will grant my two witnesses power to prophesy for one thousand two hundred and sixty days (= forty-two months or three and a half years, 12:6; 12:14; 13:5). Establishing their identity is a first priority for understanding. The signals seem mixed. First, the witnesses are the two olive trees and the two lampstands that stand before the Lord (v. 4). In Zechariah 4 this imagery is used to refer to the anointed of the Lord (= two Messiahs, kingly and priestly). In this context, such a reading is highly unlikely. Second, they have great power that sometimes sounds like Elijah (v. 5, fire that consumes foes, 2 Kings 1:10, 12; v. 6a, power to shut the sky that no rain may fall, 1 Kings 17:1; James 5:17) and sometimes sounds like Moses (v. 6b, power to turn water to blood and to smite the earth with plagues, Ex. 7–11). This echoes the Jewish belief attributed to Johannan ben Zakkai: God said to Moses, "If I send the prophet Elijah, you must both come together" (*Deuteronomy Rabbah* 10:1). In this context this identification is also unlikely. The attempt to link the two witnesses with two particular historical figures is doomed to failure. Instead, John echoes various Jewish traditions but transforms them so that the two witnesses symbolize witnessing Christians (understood as carrying out a prophetic role, cf. Acts 2:17–18, quoting Joel 2:28–29). The emphasis is on there being two witnesses (Deut. 17:6; 19:15; Matt. 18:16; John 8:17;

2 Cor. 13:1; Heb. 10:28); that is, so it would be reliable, trustworthy, and true. In the time of tribulation, the task of the church is to bear trustworthy witness.

When this is done, the witnesses both suffer persecution and experience vindication. They are killed (v. 7) and treated with contempt (vv. 8–9; to be left unburied is an act of great indignity, Tobit 2:1–7; Jer. 8:1–2), while their enemies rejoice over their demise (v. 10). But after three and a half days (= a limited time, but shorter than three and a half years) they are resuscitated (v. 11) and taken up into heaven (v. 12, the Elijah [2 Kings 2:11] and Moses [Clement of Alexandria, *Miscellanies* 6:15] allusions continue). These events of the vindication of God's witnesses are accompanied by a great earthquake (= a sign of God's presence, v. 13; 6:12; Ezek. 38:19–20). Verse 14 signals the end of the interlude: "The second woe has passed; behold, the third woe is soon to come."

The interlude (10:1–11:13) has made four points: (1) the end is near (10:1–7); (2) the prophet John speaks an authentic word from heaven (10:8–11); (3) faithful Christians are protected against apostasy during the tribulation; faithless Christians suffer for a limited time in hopes of their repentance; and (4) the task of faithful Christians during this time is to bear witness, endure the accompanying suffering, and receive the promised vindication from God. With this, the time has come for the blowing of the seventh trumpet.

The seventh trumpet is sounded, 11:15–18.

The last trumpet is a jubilant fanfare, proclaiming the enthronement of the king of kings. Loud voices in heaven announce: "The kingdom of the world has become the kingdom of our Lord and of His Christ, and He shall reign for ever and ever" (v. 15). The twenty-four elders worship God, saying: "We give thanks to Thee, Lord God Almighty, who art and who wast, that Thou hast taken thy great power and begun to reign" (v. 17). This reign involves the judgment of the dead (v. 18a). This judgment contains two parts: first, the rewarding of God's servants, the prophets and saints, and second, the destroying of the destroyers of the earth (v. 18b). The reader is here not shown God's victory. It is rather announced in heaven as part of a celestial celebration. The second vision (8:2–11:18) began with a scene in heaven designed to give assurance to the Christian hearers (8:2–6) by showing how the prayers of the saints are a catalyst for the events of the end times (vv. 3, 4–5, 6). It now ends with a proclamation of the inauguration of God's reign on earth (11:15–18). This, in effect, says again at the end of Cycle Two that the prayers of God's faithful people are answered (Matt. 6:10; Luke 18:1–8a).

In the second vision (8:2–11:18) the message is clearcut. The prayers of the saints are followed by the events of the end time. These events involve suffering, but God protects His faithful people in the great tribulation and vindicates their witness so that they ultimately share in the kingdom of God.

THE ROOTS AND ROLE OF ROMAN POWER
REVELATION 11:19–13:18

After the opening thought unit containing the letters to the seven churches in the province of Asia (2:1–3:22), there are seven visions of the end (4:1–8:1; 8:2–11:18; 11:19–13:18; 14:1–20; 15:1–16:21; 17:1–19:5; 19:6–22:5), each beginning with a scene in heaven. The first two of these visions (4:1–8:1; 8:2–11:18) focus on the tribulation, especially as it affects Christians. The gist of the two visions is that Christians will suffer during the tribulation, but God's protection will keep them from apostasy. In the third vision (11:19–13:18) the focus is on the roots and role of Roman imperial power in the sufferings of Christian believers. Revelation 11:19–13:18 is a thought unit composed of two parts: (1) 11:19, a brief opening scene in heaven designed to offer reassurance to Christian auditors prior to any "bad news" that may follow and (2) 12:1–13:18, a vision of the hostility of the dragon, the first beast, and the second beast toward the woman and her offspring. These two components must be treated in order.

11:19 = The Opening Scene in Heaven

The scene in heaven contains two ingredients: (1) a vision of the ark of the covenant within the heavenly temple (v. 19a) and (2) the accompaniments of a theophany (v. 19b).

It was ancient Jewish belief that before the Babylonians captured Jerusalem in 587 B.C., the ark of the covenant, which was kept in the Holy of Holies in the Temple, was hidden away to protect it from capture and desecration. It was, moreover, Jewish hope that the ark would reappear at the time of the eschatological restoration of the Temple (2 Macc. 2:4–8; Lives of the Prophets, "Jeremiah," 9–12). As the Lives of the Prophets, "Jeremiah," 12, puts it: "In the resurrection, the ark will rise first." When the prophet John sees the ark in the heavenly temple, it is the ultimate promise that God's love is steadfast and that the Kingdom is coming.

Accompanying the vision of the ark in the heavenly temple, there are "flashes of lightning, voices, peals of thunder, an earthquake, and heavy hail." The earth reels because it cannot stand in the awesome presence of

God (Ps. 18:7–15; cf. Ex. 9:23–25; 19:18–19; Judg. 5:4–5; 1 Kings 19:11–13; Ezek. 38:22; Joel 3:16). If the vision of the ark in the heavenly temple displayed God's promise of covenant fidelity, the accompanying theophany testifies to His active intervention in the world. Taken together, the affirmations that God is faithful and that He is active in the world offer reassurance to Christian auditors who are about to hear of their own sufferings.

12:1–13:18 = The Hostility of the Dragon and the Two Beasts

This part of the third vision is arranged not in seven but in five parts: (1) 12:1–6, the woman, the dragon, and the child; (2) 12:7–12, the dragon thrown down; (3) 12:13–17, the dragon's persecution of God's people; (4) 13:1–10, the first beast, rising out of the sea; and (5) 13:11–18, the second beast, rising out of the earth. Each must be examined in turn.

The woman, the dragon, and the child, 12:1–6.

In 12:1–6 there are three characters: a woman, a dragon, and a child. Who are they? The woman clothed with the sun, with the moon under her feet, and on her head a crown of twelve stars (v. 1) sounds like the goddess Isis (so Apuleius, *Metamorphoses* 11:3–4), but such an identification would not fit this context. In this context, she can only be the people of God who are about to give birth to the Messiah. The imagery of the Jewish people giving birth to the Messiah is found already in Isa. 26:17–18 LXX and at Qumran (1 QH 3:4).

Reference to the great red dragon (16:13; 20:2) who attempts to devour the child (vv. 3–4) may echo the combat myth of Mediterranean antiquity, either in its Greek (Apollo) or Egyptian (Horus) form, but in this context reference is to the Devil (vv. 9, 12; 2:10; 20:2, 10), Satan (v. 9; 2:9, 13, 24; 3:9; 20:2, 7), the accuser (v. 10; cf. Job 1–2; Zech. 3:1–7; 1 Chron. 21–22), and the serpent of Genesis 3 (vv. 9, 14, 15; 20:2). Whereas in the Old Testament, Satan was an angel whose role is that of accuser of humans before God in the heavenly council (Job 1–2; Zech. 3; 1 Chron. 21–22), in post-biblical Judaism Satan came to be viewed as the leader of the evil angels, an archenemy of God, who seeks not to test humans but to destroy them (1 QM 17:5; Testament of Moses 10:1; 1 QS 3–4; 1 QM 1:15–19).

Revelation assumes the developed Jewish view of Satan and then depicts his history within the Christian dispensation in terms of four stages: he is cast down from heaven to earth as a result of Christ's exaltation (12:7–12); he stands behind Roman imperial power and its persecution of Christians (chaps. 13 and 17); he will be bound for a thousand years at Christ's parousia (20:1–3); and he will be cast into the lake of fire at the last judgment (20:10).

The Satan figure represents a symbolic way of thinking about the spiritual power of evil. For Jews and early Christians, evil was more than that of individuals in the present, though it was certainly that (2 Esd. 3:21–22; 4:30; 7:48, 118–20; T. Asher 1:6, 8). It was also an accumulated bundle from the past sins of individuals whose presence is still felt (2 Bar. 23:4; 48:42–43; 56:5–6; Jubilees 3:17–35; 2 Enoch 30:15–16; 54:15–16; 2 Esd. 7:11–12). Evil was further entrenched in the institutional structures of human life (Daniel). But evil was, for them, more than all of this. It is more than individual sins in the present; it is more than the accumulation of sins from the past; it is more than corporate/structural evil. It also has a spiritual root that is the ground for all the various manifestations of human evil. This spiritual root or ground of evil in the universe was conceptualized in terms of a myth of a fallen angel, Satan (Testament of Moses 10:1; 1 QS 3:20–22). The symbolism did at least two things. First, it avoided a simplistic view of evil that was not radical enough. Second, it viewed evil, even spiritual evil, not as a fate but as the result of misused freedom.

In Revelation the evil in the human heart is exposed both by the tribulation (9:20–21; 16:9, 11, 21) and by the millenium (20:1–10). Corporate evil is destroyed in the end times (18:2, 10, 21; 19:20–21; 20:7–10), and the deception from spiritual evil is abolished at the last judgment (19:20; 20:10). Within history, however, the great red dragon is active (1 Peter 5:8; Luke 22:31). As Revelation 12–13 will show, it is he who stands behind the Roman imperial power that causes Christian suffering.

The male child who is born is he who is to rule all the nations with a rod of iron (v. 5). The allusion is to Ps. 2:9 and the Davidic Messiah. Although the great (his tail swept down a third of the stars of heaven, v. 4) red (= murderous, John 8:44) dragon tries to devour the child when the woman brings him forth, the attempt fails. The child is "caught up to God and to His throne" (v. 5). The birth of the child in this context refers not to the birth of Jesus in Bethlehem but to his exaltation to heaven, his enthronement.[14] The enthronement of the Davidic Messiah is so described in Ps. 2:7: "You are my Son, today I have begotten you". In some streams of early Christianity, Jesus' exaltation was regarded in the same way (Acts 13:33; 2:36; Rom. 1:3–4). The first scene (12:1–6) in the third vision (11:19–13:18), then, says that Satan was unsuccessful in his attempt to destroy the Messiah (Jesus).

The dragon thrown down, 12:7–12.

In 12:7–12 there are two subunits: Michael and the dragon make war in heaven (vv. 7–9) and a voice from heaven issues an announcement (vv. 10–12).

The dragon we know; who is Michael? In ancient Jewish belief,

Michael is one of the archangels, the guardian of the people of God (Dan. 12:1), who in the last days will deliver them from tribulation (1 Enoch 90:14; Assumption of Moses 10:2) and stand up for them against the kingdom of the enemy (T. Dan 6:2). Here he and his angels fight a heavenly battle (cf. Sib. Or. 3.796–808, which speaks about a battle of infantry and cavalry in the clouds) against the dragon/Satan. The dragon loses and is thrown down to the earth (Life of Adam and Eve 15–16 says about Satan's expulsion from heaven that he was thrown onto the earth; 2 Enoch 29:4–5 says, into the air) together with his angels.

Early Christians generally connected a binding/defeat of Satan with the Christ-event. Mark 3:27 (1:12–13) associates Satan's being bound with Jesus' victorious temptation. Luke 10:17–19 links Satan's fall from heaven to events within his public career, the successful mission trip of his disciples. Colossians 2:15 says Christ triumphed over the powers at the cross. John 12:31 and 16:11 assert that the ruler of this world was cast out/judged at Jesus' glorification. Revelation 12:7–12 fits into this motif, being closer to Col. 2:15 and John 12:31 than to Mark 3:27 and Luke 10:17–19 (cf. Rev. 12:11—by the blood of the Lamb). At the same time, Rev. 12:7–9 has an association with angelic warfare that is missing elsewhere in Christian sources (but is present in Dan. 10:13, 20–21; 12:1). The point is that as a result of Jesus' exaltation (12:5), Satan's power is broken in heaven (= in principle, 12:7–9).

There follows a proclamation by a voice from heaven (vv. 10–12): "Now the salvation and power and the kingdom of our God and the authority of His Christ have come, *for* the accuser of our brethren has been thrown down. . . . And they have conquered him by the blood of the Lamb and by their word of testimony, *for* they loved not their lives even unto death" (vv. 10–11). A warning follows: "Woe to you, O earth and sea, *for* the devil has come down to you in great wrath, because he knows that his time is short!" (v. 12b). The proclamation makes at least three significant points. First, the triumph of God's will in the universe is tied to the devil's being thrown down after Jesus' exaltation (= a Christus Victor motif). Second, as a result of his expulsion from heaven, the devil will cause havoc on the earth. This pain caused by an ejected Satan is nevertheless temporary. Its intensity is due to his knowledge that his time is short. The dragon's chaos is intense but brief, because he is an enemy already defeated. Third, Christians can conquer Satan's wiles by the blood of the Lamb and by their testimony. That is explained by the following phrase: "for they loved not their lives even unto death." Satan is conquered by Christians being willing to die rather than sin, just as Jesus has conquered. If scene one (12:1–6) said that Satan was unable to devour the Messiah (Jesus), scene two tells us that as a result of Jesus' exaltation, Satan's heavenly power is defeated.

He is left only with a brief time to take out his wrath on the woman and her offspring. Christians will persevere (= conquer) by their faithfulness unto death.

The dragon's presentation of God's people, 12:13–17.

In scene three (12:13–17) the dragon persecutes God's people. Three actions of the dragon shape the paragraph.

"When the dragon saw that he had been thrown down to the earth, he pursued the woman (= the people of God) who had borne the male child (= the Messiah)" (v. 13). The woman was given "the two wings of the great eagle (= a metaphor for divine help, so Deut. 32:11; Ex. 19:4; Assumption of Moses 10:8) that she might fly from the serpent into the wilderness, to a place where she is to be nourished for a time, and times, and half a time (three and a half = a limited time; cf. 12:6)" (v. 14).

"The serpent poured water like a river (= a metaphor for evil and misfortune, so Ps. 32:6; 124:4; Isa. 43:2) out of his mouth after the wo-man, to sweep her away with the flood" (v. 15). "But the earth came to the help of the woman, and the earth opened its mouth and swallowed the river (= another metaphor of divine help based on the Jewish belief that the created order cooperates with God either to punish or to bless His creatures depending on their sin or righteousness, so Wisdom of Solomon 16:24)" (v. 16).

"Then the dragon was angry with the woman (= the people of God, up to this point apparently Israel) and went off to make war on the rest of her offspring (i.e., besides the Messiah, Jesus), on those who keep the commandments of God and bear testimony to Jesus (= Christians)" (v. 17). When Satan is unable to devour the Messiah, he tries to destroy the Jewish people. When he is unable to do that, he goes off to war against the Christians. Chapter 12, then, lays the foundation for the dragon's hos-tility toward Christians. It is this wrath of a powerful spiritual being that is to be expressed by his agents, the two beasts, in chap. 13 against the followers of Jesus.

The first beast, 13:1–10.

In 13:1–10 there are two subunits: 13:1–8, the first beast that rises out of the sea, and 13:9–10, a word of exhortation.

In 13:1–8 one encounters a beast rising out of the sea. The features of the description echo Dan. 7:1–7, where the seer has a vision of four beasts rising up out of the sea (v. 3); the first like a lion (v. 4), the second like a bear (v. 5), and the third like a leopard (v. 6); the fourth beast had ten horns (v. 7). John has transposed the details of Daniel's vision so that it is one beast that he sees rising out of the sea (v. 1). Its features include similarities

to a leopard, a bear, and a lion (v. 2), and it has ten horns (= fullness of
power, v. 1). In Daniel 7, the vision of the four beasts refers to four great
empires on the stage of world history that were hostile to God's people.
Jewish thought often employed a monster as a symbol of world monarchy
hostile to God and His people (Isa. 27:1; 2 Esdras 11; Sib. Or. 2.25). It is
likely that in Revelation 13 the same pattern holds true. The beast rising
out of the sea is a reference to a world monarchy. In John's time, that would
be Rome.

Several things characterize this first beast (= Roman imperial power).
First, "to it the dragon gave his power and his throne and great authority"
(v. 2b). Behind the beast is the dragon/Satan. This scene, then, serves to
unmask Roman imperial power. It is an agent of Satan's purposes.

Second, "one of its heads seemed to have a mortal wound, but its
wound was healed" (v. 3). This is usually taken by scholars to be a reference
to the legends about Nero. Seeing that his rule had come to an end, Nero
had wavered between suicide and flight to the Parthians, where he was
popular (Suetonius, *Nero* 47). That he had considered flight led to a legend
of his flight as a fact (Sib. Or. 4.119–24). Shortly after his death, a number
of impostors claimed to be Nero: One came forward in A.D. 69 (Tacitus,
History 2.8–9; Dio Cassius, 64.9). A second appeared under Titus on the
Euphrates about A.D. 80 and was actually recognized by the Parthian king
(Tacitus, *History* 1.2; Suetonius, *Nero* 57). A third appeared about A.D. 88,
supported by the Parthians (Tacitus, *History* 1.2; Suetonius, *Nero* 57). Belief
that Nero was alive continued at least to the time of Trajan. Dio Chrysostom (*Orations* 21.10) says this: "The great majority do believe that he is
[i.e., Nero is still alive], although in a certain sense he died not once but
often along with those who had been firmly convinced that he was still
alive."

This formed the backdrop for two very different legends. On the one
hand, some believed that Nero, still alive, would come at the head of the
Parthian army and destroy Rome and her empire (Tacitus, *History* 2.8–9;
Suetonius, *Nero* 57; Dio Cassius, 64.9; Sib. Or. 4.137–39; 8.65–72; 8.139–
59). On the other hand, others believed that Nero would return as persecutor of God's people. This belief took two forms. According to the first,
Nero is an evil figure analogous to Antiochus Epiphanes in Daniel, that
is, the last persecutor (Sib. Or. 5.93–110; 5.137–54; 5.214–27; 5.361–85;
Lactantius, *How Persecutors Died* 2). According to the second view, Nero
is the embodiment of Belial/Beliar, that is, the incarnation of Satan, the
Antichrist (Ascension of Isaiah 4:1–2; Sib. Or. 3.63–64). In Revelation one
finds echoes of more than one form of the Nero legend.

In 13:3, "one of its (= the beast's) heads seemed to have a mortal
wound, but its mortal wound was healed," makes Nero a demonic imita-
tion of "the Lamb standing, as though it had been slain" (5:6). Indeed in

Revelation 12–13 the counter kingdom of the dragon, the first beast, and the second beast (= the false prophet) is set over against God, the Lamb, and the true prophet. Reality has its counterfeit! The seven heads (vv. 1, 3) refer to the complete number of Roman emperors. The ten horns refer to its fullness of power. The beast, then, is Roman imperial power, of which Nero is the typical embodiment.

Third, "people worshiped the dragon . . . and they worshiped the beast" because of its power (v. 4). Indeed, "all who dwell on the earth will worship it, every one whose name has not been written before the foundation of the world in the book of life (Ex. 32:33; Phil. 4:3; Rev. 3:5; 17:8; 20:12, 15; 21:17) of the Lamb that was slain" (v. 8). The political unity of the Roman empire was expressed through the common bond of imperial worship.[15] Some background will assist our understanding.

Pliny the Elder (*Natural History* 2.19) says that to enroll rulers among the deities is the most ancient method of showing gratitude for their benefactions. Ovid (*Tristia* 2.53–60) lists as acts of devotion that true citizens should pay to their emperor, the offering of incense and paying vows to the emperor as tokens of loyalty to the state. Nowhere was this mind-set more avidly embraced than in the province of Asia. It was the province of Asia that first requested from Augustus the privilege of worshiping him (Dio Cassius, 51.20.7; Suetonius, *Augustus* 52). As a result, during Augustus's lifetime a temple in his honor was erected in Pergamum (Tacitus, *Annals* 4.37). In A.D. 26 Smyrna won the right to erect a temple in honor of Tiberius, beating out Sardis and Laodicea (Tacitus, *Annals* 4.55). Ephesus already had temples to Julius Caesar and Claudius, but in Domitian's time engaged in major building projects that were related to the emperor cult.

Two building projects in particular reflect the mentality of the time. The first was the Temple of the Sebastoi (= the so-called temple of Domitian at the upper end of Curetes Street). This was probably dedicated to the cult of the Flavian emperors, Vespasian, Titus, and Domitian. It was built on an artificial platform about 300 feet long and 200 feet wide. On the north side of the platform there was a three-story stoa. The second-story colonnade was ornamented with figures of deities on each column, creating an array of gods and goddesses visible to passersby below the temple.

> The symbolism was powerful: The deities of the empire supported and protected the emperors who were worshiped in the temple above. Conversely, the emperors were the unifying element that brought the gods and goddesses together. In this sense, the emperors had become the focal point in the relationship between the human and divine realms.[16]

This temple, though built at Ephesus, was a provincial temple. It was not built as a municipal or individual project but was established by the provincial council of Asia after approval by the Senate in Rome. It therefore reflects the developments in the province of Asia at the end of the first century A.D.

A second building project in Ephesus in Domitian's era was the bath-gymnasium complex in the harbor area. It was built by the Ephesians for Domitian about the time the province was building the Temple of the Sebastoi. It was built to honor Domitian as Zeus Olympius with his own Olympic festival.

> Together the Temple of the Sebastoi and the bath-gymnasium complex near the harbor reflect significant trends in late first-century Ephesus. The worship of the emperors altered two major areas of the city. . . . Equally important, the worship of the emperors gave a new coherence to the city by creating a link between these two areas. The imperial cult in effect provided a fresh unity to the entire city.[17]

The trend continued into the time of Trajan. At Ephesus archeologists have recovered fragments of a statue of Trajan that is twice life-size. The stone base has an inscription that calls him *theou huion* (= son of God). At the right foot of Trajan is a globe, a symbol that says that the whole world is subject to him.[18] It was the worship of Roman imperial power, embraced eagerly by the citizens of Asia, that was the focal point of the entire culture.

The Jews, of course, were the exception. Because of the help Julius Caesar had received from Antipater during the Alexandrian campaign and his generally friendly relations with Hyrcanus II and the Jews of Palestine, he favored the Diaspora Jews in his legislation. He formalized and legalized what had until then been unwritten convention that the Jews should have religious liberty in the empire (Josephus, *Antiquities*, 14.10.1–8 § 185–216). Augustus continued this policy (Philo, *Legation* 156–58). In A.D. 2 or 3, Augustus sent an edict to the proconsul in Asia, setting out Jewish rights in full. They were to be posted on the temple of the imperial cult in Ancyra (*Antiquities* 16.6.2 § 162–65). Augustus's policies were reaffirmed by Claudius (Josephus, *Antiquities* 19.5.2 § 278–85). Except for the last few years of Hadrian's reign, this policy continued unaltered for three centuries. As part of their religious freedom, Jews were allowed to pray for the emperor in their own places of worship as an alternative to offering sacrifice in the emperor cult. The Christians, unfortunately, had no such exception or protection.

Fourth, the first beast blasphemes God (v. 6; cf. Dan. 7:25; 11:36; 2 Thess. 2:4; Ascension of Isaiah 4:6; Sib. Or. 5:33–34) and makes war on the saints, conquering them (v. 7). To a Christian like John of Patmos, any claim such as that designating Trajan as "son of God" would be regarded as blasphemy. Any willingness on Rome's part to accept such veneration would have been seen as blasphemous. This blasphemous Roman imperial power, moreover, is "allowed to make war on the saints and to conquer them" (v. 7). Keep in mind that in these visions, John is seeing what lies in the future for his auditors (2:10; 3:10). When the idolatrous Roman imperial culture realizes the incompatibility of its own ethos and that of the Christians, persecution will result for Christians who do not worship the emperor.

In 13:9–10 there is a word of exhortation. "If anyone has an ear, let him hear" (v. 9). Hear what?

> If anyone is to be taken captive, to captivity he goes;
> If anyone slays with the sword, with the sword must he be slain (v. 10a).

God's control of history is a fact for persecuted and persecutor alike. Suffering for the persecuted is not without God's sovereign will, just as the just punishment of the persecutor resides within God's overriding purpose. "Here is a call for the endurance and faith of the saints" (v. 10b).

The second beast, 13:11–18.

In 13:11–18 there are also two components: a vision of a second beast rising out of the earth (vv. 11–17) and another word of exhortation (v. 18). The second beast makes its appearance in 13:11–17, rising out of the earth. It has two horns (= great strength) and speaks like a dragon (= its ultimate authority is the dragon of chap. 12). "It exercises all the authority of the first beast in its presence, and makes the earth and its inhabitants worship the first beast" (v. 12). This second beast is either the local priests of the emperor cult or the provincial council responsible for enforcing emperor worship throughout Asia. It represents the sponsor of the worship of Roman imperial power, whoever that may be.

Worship of the beast involves two things: (1) making an image for the first beast (v. 14) and worshiping that image (v. 15), and (2) being marked on the right hand or the forehead with the name or number of the first beast (vv. 16–17).

One of the most usual forms of imperial worship took place before the statue of the emperor, before which honor could be rendered as a mark of loyalty. Such practices had a long history (Dan. 3:15, the Persian king; Plutarch, *Gracchus* 18.2, the Gracchi; Tacitus, *Annals* 1.10.5, Augustus; Philo, *Gaius* 29, 188; 30, 198; 43, 346, Caligula; Dio Cassius 62.18.3; 67.8.1, Nero). They persisted into the time of Domitian (Suetonius, *Nero* 23.2) and Trajan (Pliny, *Epistles* 10.96). Pliny says of his procedure for dealing with those accused of being Christians:

> All who denied that they were or had been Christians were discharged, because they called upon the gods and did reverence . . . to your image which had been brought forward for this purpose.

It is this type of practice to which Rev. 13:15 refers.

Another form of devotion mentioned by Rev. 13:16–17 is the marking on the right hand or forehead with the name or number of the first beast. Religious tattooing was widespread in antiquity as a way of indicating one's devotion to a deity (Herodotus 2.113; 3 Macc. 2.29; Lucian, *Syrian Goddess* 59). Jews had an equivalent practice. They wore the tephillin on the left hand and the head (Deut. 6:8). Here the marking with the name or number of the beast is a parody of the sealing of the servants of God in Rev. 7:3 ("Do not harm the earth or the sea or the trees till we have sealed the servants of our God upon their foreheads"). Adherence to the first beast, sponsored by the second beast, takes the form both of worship before the first beast's statue and of being marked with his name or number.

One way the second beast facilitates emperor worship is to use deceiving signs (vv. 13–14). Such an outburst of false miracles was expected in the end time (4 Ezra 5:4; Sib. Or. 3.63–70; Mark 13:22; 2 Thess. 2:9; Ascension of Isaiah 4:10). Certain of the deceptive signs are mentioned: the second beast makes fire come down from heaven to earth in the sight of men (v. 13b); and he gives breath to the image of the beast so that it can even speak (v. 15a).

The fire sign is obviously, for John of Patmos, a counterfeit of Elijah's miracle on Mount Carmel (1 Kings 18:38; 2 Kings 1:10, 12; Luke 9:54). The second beast is a false prophet (cf. Rev. 16:13; 19:20). The fire sign may also be based upon actual occurrences. Contrived religious wonders were not unusual in antiquity.[19] One type had to do with fire. Hippolytus (*Refutation* 4.35–36) speaks about magicians' ability to produce a fiery bolt through the air. Plutarch's criticism of rulers who imitate God's thunder, lightning, and sunbeams (*Moralia* 780F) indicates that some must surely have done precisely this. Ancient authors tell us about machines to simulate thunder (Hippolytus, *Refutation* 4:32; Julius Pollux, *Onomasticon* 4.130). They also tell about machines to simulate lightning (Julius Pollux, *Onomasticon* 4.130). Dio Cassius (59.28.6) connects such machines with the Roman emperors. For example, Gaius "had a contrivance by which he gave answering peals when it thundered and sent return flashes when it lightened. Likewise, whenever a bolt fell, he would in turn hurl a javelin at a rock." It may very well be that in the emperor cult such mechanisms were used to produce deceptive signs that would elicit people's devotion to Roman imperial power.

The sign involving an image that could move and/or speak also belonged to antiquity's horde of religious deceptions. The magician Simon claims to have animated lifeless things (*Ps. Clementine Recognitions* 3.47). Many assumed that statues could speak. Suetonius (*Gaius* 57.1) tells without explanation about a statue of Jupiter at Rome that laughed. The Christian apologist Athenagoras (*Supplication for the Christians* 27) interprets the ability of statues of pagan heroes to give oracles and to heal the sick to demonic influence. The pagan Lucian (*Alexander the False Prophet* 26) attributes it to human deception:

> As he [Alexander] wished to astonish the crowd still more, he promised to produce the god talking—delivering oracles in person without a prophet. It was no difficult matter for him to fasten crane's windpipes together and pass them through the head. . . . Then he answered the questions through someone else, who spoke into the tube from the outside, so that the voice issued from his canvas Asclepius.

The Christian Hippolytus (*Refutation* 4.41) likewise explains the mechanics of the deception:

> It presents the appearance of a skull, which seems to speak when the contrivance operates . . . when having procured the windpipe of a crane, or some other long-necked animal, and attaching it covertly to the skull, the accomplice utters what he wishes.

It is this type of deceptive sign that Rev. 13:15 attributes to the imperial cult as one of its false signs aimed at eliciting devotion to the emperor.

Another way the second beast seeks to make the world worship the first beast (= Roman imperial power) is through persecution. This involves both capital punishment (v. 15b, "cause those who would not worship the image of the beast to be slain") and economic penalties (v. 17, "so that no one could buy or sell unless he has the mark" of the beast). Pliny (*Epistles* 10.96) shows that in the time of Trajan failure to worship the image of the emperor could result in capital punishment. Failure to participate in banquets associated with reverence for the imperial power would certainly result in economic reprisals. One's economic well-being, John warns about the predicted future, will be tied to devotion to the first beast (= Roman imperial power).

A word of exhortation (13:18) concludes the fifth and final scene of the vision: "This calls for wisdom: let those who have understanding reckon the number of the beast, for it is a human number, its number is six hundred sixty-six." Attempts to interpret this phase usually take one of two directions. On the one hand, some see the number 666 as a code for a name of a specific individual. In ancient times, letters of the alphabet served as numbers. Thus every name yielded a number. For example, at Pompeii (not later than A.D. 79) a wall scribbling reads: "Amerimnus thought upon his lady Harmonia for good. The number of her honorable name is 45." Another reads: "I love her whose number is 545."[20] In the Sib. Or. 1.324–6, the name of Jesus is given as 888.[21] Given this ancient practice, numerous interpreters have attempted to find the name of the person behind the number 666. The history of interpretation offers well over one hundred different interpretations among modern British writers alone.[22] The seeming impossibility to decipher 666 as a name of an individual leads to the second tack taken. Other scholars have regarded 666 not as the name of an individual but merely as a symbolic number. Among the ancients numbers have symbolic value. If the number 7 implies perfection, the number 6 conveys imperfection. Raise it to a series and it produces an imperfection of which there can be no greater. The number 666, then, symbolizes the ultimate in imperfection. Whatever is described by such a number is flawed, fatally flawed. The prophet of Patmos places an evaluation upon Roman imperial power as symbolized by Nero: 666, the ultimate in imperfection, fatally flawed. Those who have wisdom will know this!

Revelation 11:19–13:18 has given its auditors an exposé of Roman imperial power and the apparatus of the emperor cult that promotes it. Both empire and emperor cult are representatives of the great red dragon. Behind Rome's actions is the power of the devil delegated to the empire and its false religion. Any suffering Christians may experience from Rome because they resist Roman imperial culture as idolatrous is due to the hostility of the dragon.

The attitude toward the state that one encounters in Revelation is that toward a state that has overstepped its bounds. In Daniel one finds the posture that God's people should submit to the authority God has given to the state (be it pagan or not) up to the point at which they are forced to compromise their religion (Dan. 2:37–38; 3:18, 28; 4:17; chap. 6). The same attitude is found elsewhere in Jewish apocalypses (e.g., 1 Enoch 85–90; Testament of Moses). Early Christians followed the Jewish lead: "According as the State remains within its limits or transgresses them, the Christian will describe it as the servant of God or as the instrument of the Devil."[23] On the one hand, Rom. 13:1–7 and 1 Peter 2:13–17 take a positive stance toward the state. The state here is the instrument of God, whether it recognizes God or not. Acts 19:31, moreover, refers to the Asiarchs as friends of Paul. They represented a political institution alongside the Roman provincial government and the Greek municipal government. They were the council of the cities of Asia whose duties were religious as well as political. Under the empire they maintained the cult of the reigning emperor in various cities.[24] They are mentioned in Acts to show that officers of the imperial cult did not regard Paul as an enemy. The narrator of Acts does not refer to them in a way that assumes their demonic character. On the other hand, Revelation 12–13 and 17–18 take a negative attitude toward the state. The state here is seen as the instrument of Satan because it has abused the authority given it by God and has demanded what belongs to God alone. When the state assumes the role of God, wisdom says it is rooted in satanic power. From John's perspective, all who support and promote the religion of such a totalitarian state, be they in or out of the church, are agents of the dragon.

Visions one (4:1–8:1) and two (8:2–11:18) focus on the tribulation in general terms as it impacts primarily Christians. Vision three (11:19–13:18) speaks about the tribulation as it impacts Christians in concrete, particular terms. It pictures the persecution that Christians will suffer at the hands of Roman imperial power because they do not participate in the cult of the emperor. In visions four (14:1–20) and five (15:1–16:21) the focus is on the tribulation as it impacts unbelievers especially, as judgment within history. It is to vision four (14:1–20) that we now turn.

THE SEVEN AGENTS OF JUDGMENT
REVELATION 14:1–20

The bulk of the Revelation to John consists of seven visions of the end times (4:1–8:1; 8:2–11:18; 11:19–13:18; 14:1–20; 15:1–16:21; 17:1–19:5; 19:6–22:5). The first two visions focus on the tribulation viewed in general terms, especially as it impacts believers. They give assurance that God is in control and that He will protect His people from spiritual apostasy during their sufferings. The third makes clear in concrete terms (a) that the tribulation for Christians will consist of persecution by Roman imperial power because Christians will not participate in the emperor cult and (b) that behind these sufferings lies the wrath of the great red dragon/Satan.

The fourth (14:1–20) and fifth (15:1–16:21) visions of the shift of the ages focus on judgment, within history and at the end of history, especially as it affects Rome and its sympathizers.[25] Here the tribulation is viewed as judgment at the end of, but still within, history that is a prelude to the final judgment, when history is no more. Visions four and five are virtually synonymous (repetition with variation), just as were visions one and two (4:1–8:1; 8:2–11:18).

Just as with all seven visions of the end time in Revelation, vision four (14:1–20) begins with a scene in heaven that is designed to give reassurance to its Christian auditors. Revelation 14:1–20, then, is organized in two parts: (1) an opening scene in heaven (14:1–5) and (2) the seven agents of judgment (14:6–20). Each must be examined in turn.

14:1–5 = Opening Scene in Heaven

The opening scene in heaven has three components: a vision (v. 1), an audition (vv. 2–3a), and an explanation (vv. 3b–5).

What is the vision? The prophet says: "Then I looked, and lo, on Mount Zion (= the heavenly city of Jerusalem, Heb. 12:22; 5 Ezra 2:42–48) stood the Lamb (= Christ, 5:6, 8, 12); 6:1, 16; 7:14, 17; 8:1), and with him a hundred and forty-four thousand (= the church, 7:3–8; cf. Heb. 12:23, the assembly of the firstborn who are enrolled in heaven) who had his name and his Father's name written on their foreheads (7:3, a sealing that is parodied by the mark of the beast in 13:16–17)" (v. 1). What is seen, then, is a proleptic vision (= a vision in the present of a future reality) of the redeemed church.

What is the audition? John says: "And I heard a voice from heaven like the sound of many waters (1:15) and like the sound of loud thunder (4:5); the voice I heard was like the sound of harpers playing on their harps, and they sing a new song (5:9) before the throne (4:2) and before the four living creatures (4:6b) and before the elders (4:4)" (vv. 2–3a). The voice from heaven is strong/loud but melodious. It is the sound of the hundred forty-four thousand singing a new song, celebrating the new deliverance from God (5:9–10; Ex. 15:1; Ps. 33:3; 40:3; 96:1; 98:1; 149:1; Isa. 42:10). By means of this vision, the Christian auditors can listen even now to the song they will hereafter join in singing.

What is the explanation? First, there is a general statement of boundaries. "No one could learn that song except the hundred forty-four thousand who had been redeemed from earth" (v. 3b). Only the redeemed are able to sing the new song (= only the 144,000 who have experienced the new deliverance can give thanks for it; cf. Luke 7:47[26]). From the point of view of John of Patmos, the heavenly Jerusalem is not characterized by total inclusiveness. It is rather an exclusive community. After all, without boundaries, there is no community.

Second, there is a statement of characteristics of those included in the heavenly Jerusalem: "It is these who have not defiled themselves with women, for they are chaste (virgins, *parthenoi* = masculine plural); it is these who follow the Lamb wherever he goes; these have been redeemed from mankind as firstfruits for God and the Lamb, and in their mouth no lie was found, for they were spotless" (vv. 4–5).

The first characteristic of the hundred forty-four thousand is the most difficult to understand. What does it mean for the hundred forty-four thousand to be virgins? Is this a call for universal Christian sexual asceticism? Several items of background information will assist us in our answer.

In ancient Israel, men involved in war followed special rules (Deut. 23:9–11), one of which was abstinence from sexual relations (1 Sam. 21:5; 2 Sam. 11:1). A ready warrior, then, is one who lives as a virgin.

In the Old Testament, the marriage relationship is often used as an analogy for the covenant between Yahweh and Israel. Faithfulness to Yahweh is described as sexual faithfulness; unfaithfulness/idolatry is depicted as spiritual adultery/harlotry (Isa. 1:21; Jer. 2:20; 3:8–9; Ezek. 16:15–22; Hos. 4:15). Revelation 17:1–5 continues this mind-set, depicting Rome as a harlot (= faithless to God) with whom others have committed fornication (= spiritual adultery/idolatry). Revelation 19:7–9 and 21:2, 9, moreover, portray the church as the bride of Christ. It would seem that either or both these items of background information could provide the clue for 14:4. Either the virgins are those who are ready spiritual warriors, abstaining from any involvement in spiritual adultery, or they are the pure future bride of Christ, abstaining from any defilement of improper alliances prior to her wedding day (Rev. 21:2; 2 Cor. 11:2; Eph. 5:27) or both. If a choice has to be made, judging by the references elsewhere in Revelation to the church as the bride of Christ, it is likely the image of a pure virgin awaiting her wedding day.[27] A symbolic reading of "virgins" is confirmed by the fact that Philo (*On the Cherubim* 49–50) uses the grammatically masculine term "virgins" in a metaphorical sense for God's people, male and female. The first characteristic of those included in the company of heaven is spiritual faithfulness (= abstinence from idolatry; cf. 1 John 5:20–21).

The other traits are less difficult to grasp. "Those who follow the Lamb wherever he goes" are those who are willing to follow him even unto death (2:10; cf. John 13:36; 21:19, 22[28]). Those "redeemed from mankind as firstfruits (= the first sheaf of the grain harvest, presented to God in gratitude for the pledge of the full harvest to come, Ex. 34:22; Lev. 23:15–22; Num. 28:26; Deut. 16:9–12) for God and the Lamb" are the initial converts in the churches addressed, who have been set free from bondage to pagan society (1 Peter 1:14–19; 4:3–4) and its values as a pledge of many other Christians yet to come (James 1:18). Those described by "in their mouth no lie was found (21:8; 22:15), for they are spotless (3:4; cf. Eph. 5:27)" are Christians who stand by their Christian confession even unto death. Not only is the heavenly city not all-inclusive, it is inclusive only for those who break with their non-Christian culture, abstain from idolatry, and hold fast their Christian confession unto death in the face of demands to assimilate to Roman imperial culture. For those who meet the entrance requirements, the vision of the heavenly city with its inhabitants singing a new song in the presence of the Lamb is a reassurance that their future is secure.

The opening scene in heaven (14:1–5) of vision four (14:1–20) has offered a number of images of the church: the true Israel (= the 144,000; cf. 7:4); the redeemed from the earth (cf. 1:5; 5:9); the pure bride of Christ (cf. 21:2, 9; 19:7); the followers of the Lamb. Elsewhere in Revelation, other images are used: for example, the temple (11:1–2); the new Jerusalem (21:2, 10); the saints (5:8; 11:18; 13:7, 10; 14:12; 16:6; 17:6; 18:24; 19:8;

20:9); priests of God (5:10; 7:15). All these images reflect the ecclesiastical ideal. The ecclesiastical reality is reflected in the letters to the seven churches (2:1–3:22). In 14:1–5, the church in the world is offered a picture of the church in heaven as a basis for confidence amid the trials of this age.

14:6–20 = The Seven Agents of Judgment

In 14:6–20 there are seven announcements of God's judgment, starting with that on Babylon (v. 8) and those with the mark of the beast (vv. 9–10) that comes at the end of, but within, history. These announcements are made by seven agents, six of whom are specified as angels (vv. 6, 8, 9, 15, 17, 18). The only exception comes in v. 14 where the agent is called "one like a son of man." Apocalyptic symbolism often uses figures one step below the designated subjects on the chain of being to describe them. For example, beasts are used to talk about human empires (Dan. 7:3–8; 8:20–26); a man, or one having the appearance of a man, is used to speak about an angel (Dan. 8:15–16; 9:21; 10:5, 18; 12:6–7). Given the context of 14:6–20 (six angels on either side of the "one like a son of man") and given the tendency of apocalyptic to describe subjects with figures one step below them on the chain of being, it seems likely that the "one like a son of man" in 14:14 is yet a seventh angel, not Christ. If so, then the seven agents of judgment are actually the seven angels of judgment.

In contrast to most of the Old Testament where angelology is relatively undeveloped, in Jewish and Christian apocalyptic literature angels are major characters.[29]

Their nature. Angels are creatures (Ascension of Isaiah 7:21; 8:4–5) who are numerous (1 Enoch 60:1–4; 2 Bar. 59:11; Ascension of Isaiah 7:14–17; Apocalypse of Paul 14), who serve in God's presence (Testament of Abraham 20:17–18; Ascension of Isaiah 11:31–32). They belong to many different categories: for example, seven archangels (Tobit 12:15; 1 Enoch 20:1–8; 81:5; 87:1; 90:22), Seraphim, Cherubim, and Opannim (1 Enoch 71:7–11; 61:10; 40:2–10), patron angels of various nations, such as Israel (Dan. 10:21; 11:1; 12:1); angels who are in charge of the world (1 Enoch 60:11–24). Jubilees 2:2 puts it concisely.

> On the first day He created the heavens, which are above,
> and the earth, and the waters and all of the spirits which
> minister before Him:
> the angels of His presence,
> and the angels of sanctification,
> and the angels of the spirit of fire,
> and the angels of the spirit of the clouds and darkness and snow and hail and
>   frost,
> and the angels of resoundings and thunder and lightning,

and the angels of the spirits of cold and heat and winter and springtime and
harvest and summer,
and all of the spirits of His creatures which are in heaven and on earth.

They have a glorious appearance (Testament of Abraham 2:6; Ascension
of Isaiah 7:2). They are sometimes said to have feelings (2 Bar. 67:1–3
[pain]; 1 Enoch 13:3 [fear]; Testament of Abraham 3:11–12 [sympathy]).

Their functions. Although they are created to be subordinate to God
and His servants, some angels are disobedient (1 Enoch 16:2; 9:6; 2 Enoch
7:3; 29:4–5; Life of Adam and Eve 15:3; Jub. 10:8; 11:5). Among the obedi-
ent angels, their functions include: serving as messengers (Testament of
Abraham 2:9–10), guides (T. Levi 3), revealers (1 Enoch 60:11), and interpreters (2 Bar. 56:1; 71:2–3; 5 Ezra 2:44–47); acting as guardians of nations
(Dan. 10:13–21; 1 Enoch 89:59–60; Jub. 15:31–32; T. Levi 5–6) and of
individuals (Apocalypse of Paul 7), performing such roles as that of inter-
cessor (1 Enoch 15:2; 39:5; 40:9; 89:76; 104:1; T. Levi 3:5); serving as warriors against nations (2 Bar. 63:5–11) and evil angels alike (1 QM 17:5–8;
Apocalypse of Paul 14); and acting as agents of judgment of humans (2 Bar.
51:11–12; Testament of Abraham 11:6; 20:14–17; Sib. Or. 2.215–35, 285;
Apocalypse of Peter 6) and of evil angels (1 Enoch 54).
Revelation assumes much of the apocalyptic view of angels.

Their nature. They are creatures (Rev. 19:10; 22:8–9) who are not to
be worshiped (cf. Col. 2:18). They themselves dwell in God's presence and
worship Him (Rev. 4:10; 8:2). They are numerous: "Then I looked, and I
heard around the throne and the living creatures and the elders the voice of
many angels, numbering myriads of myriads and thousands of thousands"
(5:11). They belong to many different categories: for example, twenty-four
elders (= the heavenly council, Rev. 4:4; 14:3), the four living creatures
(= the cherubim, Rev. 4:6b-8), angels of judgment (Rev. 7:1; 9:14–15).
Their appearance is glorious (10:1). At no point in Revelation, however,
is anything ever said about angels' feelings.

Their functions. Above all, in Revelation angels have a revelatory function (Rev. 1:1–3; 17:1–3, 7; 21:9–10; 22:6, 16). They also function as guardians of God's people (7:1; 8:3–4). They also act as warriors against the
dragon (12:7–9), the beast, and the false prophet (19:14, 19–20). They fur-
thermore act as agents of judgment (20:1–3). When angels act as agents of
judgment in Revelation, at least four different images are used: judicial
imagery, where angels announce judgment (10:1–9; 14:6–11; 18:1–3,
21–24; 19:17–18); agricultural imagery, where angels gather the eschatological harvest (14:15–20); pathological imagery, where angels deliver

plagues (15:1; 16:1); and military imagery, where angels act as warriors (12:7–9; 19:14, 19–21). In Revelation 14:6–20 the seven angels are agents of judgment. Their role is conceptualized in terms of two images: judicial, where they announce judgment (14:6–7, 8, 9–11), and agricultural, where they gather the eschatological harvest (14:14–16, 17–20). The former image is used for judgment at the end of, but within, history; the latter image, for the last judgment. With this background, one is now ready to read about the seven angelic agents of judgment in Rev. 14:6–20.

The pattern of the seven agents of judgment is the same as that in the next vision (15:1–16:21). There is first a series of three agents (vv. 6–7, 8, 9–12), followed by an interlude (the two voices, v. 13), and concluded by the final four agents (vv. 14–20). The series of the final four agents of judgment is broken into two groups of two each (vv. 14–16, 17–20).

The first angel, 14:6–7.

In 14:6–7 one meets the first angel of judgment.

> Then I saw another angel flying in midheaven, with an eternal gospel to proclaim to those who dwell upon the earth, to every nation and tribe and tongue and people; and he said with a loud voice, "Fear God and give Him glory for the hour of His judgment has come; and worship Him who made heaven and earth, the sea and the fountains of water."

The "gospel" proclaimed here is the good news that God is intervening to judge. It is a proclamation aimed at a universal audience. It calls for humans to worship the creator (Acts 14:15).

The second angel, 14:8.

In 14:8 one encounters the second angel of judgment: "Another angel . . . followed, saying, 'Fallen, fallen is Babylon the great (Isa. 21:9; Jer. 51:8), she who made all nations drink the wine of her impure passion (17:2).'" Babylon here is a symbol for imperial Rome (2 Bar. 11:1; Sib. Or. 5.143, 159; 1 Peter 5:13). Drinking the "wine of her impure passion" refers to all nations being involved in her idolatry. Idolatrous Rome, so the angelic announcement goes, is fallen. This is her judgment within history (= the tribulation for Rome).

The third angel, 14:9–12.

In 14:9–12 one is confronted with yet a third angel of judgment. His announcement runs thus: "If anyone worships the beast and its image (13:4, 8, 12, 15), and receives a mark on his forehead or on his hand (13:16–17), he also shall drink the wine of God's wrath (Isa. 51:17, 22; Jer. 25:15), poured unmixed into the cup of His anger, and he shall be tormented with fire and sulphur (19:20; 20:10; 21:8; 1 Enoch 90:26–27; 4 Ezra 7:36; Luke

16:24) in the presence of the holy angels and the Lamb." It is not just Roman imperial power that suffers God's wrath; it is also those who have participated in emperor worship.

Wrath associated with God (as opposed to the dragon's wrath, 12:12) is mentioned in Rev. 6:16–17; 11:18; 14:10, 19; 15:1, 7; 16:1, 19; and 19:15.

Its source is sometimes God (14:19; 15:1; cf. 1 Enoch 5:9; 55:3; 1 QS 4:12; Testament of Moses 10:3) and sometimes the Lamb (6:16–17). It is sometimes pictured as a theophany that sends the cosmos reeling (6:12–17; cf. 2 Bar. 48:17); sometimes as a cup or bowl of anger poured out (14:10; 16:1, 19; cf. Job 21:20; Ps. 75:8; Isa. 51:17; Jer. 25:15; 49:12; Ezek. 23:32–34; Zech. 12:2); and sometimes as a winepress to be trodden down (14:19; 19:15; cf. Isa. 63:6; Lam. 1:15).

The objects of wrath are the inhabitants of the earth (11:18; 14:8, 19; 16:1, 19; 18:3; 19:15; cf. 2 Bar. 29:1; 1 QM 15:1), the earth and the cosmos (8:12–13; 16:1; cf. 1 Enoch 1:7; 2 Bar. 27:6–7; T. Levi 4:1; Testament of Moses 10:4–5), and Satan with his followers (14:9–10; 20:19–20; cf. 1 QM 18:1; 1 Enoch 18:16; 19:1, 28; 69:28; 90:21, 24).

The time of God's wrath is twofold: both within history (15:1–16:16; cf. 4 Ezra; 2 Bar.; 1 Enoch 67; Rom. 1:18) and at the end of history (14:10, 19; 16:17–21; cf. 1 QM 1:12; 4 Ezra 5:1; 2 Bar. 25–26; 1 Enoch 45:2; 1 Thess. 1:9–10).

There are multiple purposes of God's wrath. Within history, it functions to lead to repentance (9:20; 16:9, 11, 21; cf. 2 Bar. 13:9–10; Testament of Moses 1:18; Dan. 4; Hermas, "Vision," 4.2.5), to test believers' faith (3:10; cf. 1 QM 3:13–16; 17:8–9), and as retribution (16:15–17; 18:4–8). At the end of history, it serves to settle accounts (11:18; cf. 4 Ezra 7:42; 1 Enoch 50:4; 2 Bar. 42:2).

The agents who execute God's wrath are sometimes the Messiah (19:11–16; cf. 1 Enoch 46:4; 69:27; 4 Ezra 12:31–37; Ascension of Isaiah 9:4–5), sometimes angels (15:1–16:21; 14:6–20; cf. T. Levi 3:2–3; 1 Enoch 66:1–2; Matt. 13:30), and sometimes God Himself (16:17–21). In Revelation 14, wrath comes from God, is imaged as a cup and a winepress, and is carried out by angelic agents at the end of history as a settling of accounts.

There is a clear shift at 14:9 from judgment within history (= the fall of Rome, v. 8) to judgment at the end of history, the last judgment. The effects of the last judgment, which is an expression of God's wrath (= resistance to evil), are permanent: "The smoke of their torment goes up for ever and ever; and they have no rest, day or night, these worshipers of the beast and its image, and whoever receives the mark of its name." Does Revelation subscribe to universalism (= all will eventually be saved), to annihilation (= the wicked will be destroyed and cease to exist), or to an eternal punishment?

An answer lies in the phrase in v. 11, "for ever and ever." Revelation 4:10, 10:6, and 15:7 say God on the throne is the one "who lives for ever and ever." Revelation 1:18 has the risen Christ say: "I died, and behold I am alive for evermore." Revelation 11:15 has voices in heaven say: "The kingdom of the world has become the kingdom of our Lord and of His Christ, and he (Christ) shall reign for ever and ever." Revelation 22:5 says of the fate of the righteous: "They shall reign for ever and ever."

Two passages in the Apocalypse of John speak about the fate of the wicked in the same terms. Revelation 20:10 says that the devil, the beast, and the false prophet will be tormented day and night "for ever and ever," and 14:9–11 says of those who worship the beast and have his mark, "the smoke of their torment goes up for ever and ever." Whatever the phrase "for ever and ever" means in one of these references, it means in all. It cannot imply universalism[30]; it is not taken naturally to mean annihilation[31]; it most naturally means, in the Apocalypse of John, everlasting punishment.

The interlude, 14:13

After the first three agents of judgment make their proclamations, there is an interlude with two voices (14:13). The first is simply "a voice from heaven." It says, "Blessed are the dead who die in the Lord henceforth." That is, the Christians who are to be martyred for their witness are blessed (= to be congratulated) in contrast to those who have worshiped the beast and will share in Rome's torment for ever and ever. The first heavenly voice's beatitude is reinforced by the Spirit: "Blessed indeed, that they may rest from their labors, for their deeds follow them." Such a beatitude has power because it comes from two heavenly witnesses (Deut. 19:15; 1 Tim. 5:19).

There follow the final four angelic agents of judgment (vv. 14–20). The series consists of two subunits, vv. 14–16 and vv. 17–20.

Verses 14–16	*Verses 17–20*
The fourth agent holds a sharp sickle.	The sixth agent holds a sharp sickle.
Another angel calls, "Put in your sickle, and reap."	Another angel calls, "Put in your sickle, and gather."
So he swung his sickle on the earth.	So he swung his sickle on the earth.

The fourth and fifth angels, 14:14–16.

Let us examine the first subunit (vv. 14–16). One like a son of man (= an angel, the fourth in the series) holds a sharp sickle in his hand. Another angel (= the fifth in the series) comes out of the heavenly temple (11:19) and calls to the fourth angel: "Put in your sickle, and reap, for the hour to reap has come, for the harvest of the earth is fully ripe" (Joel 3:13). So the one like a son of man swung his sickle and "the earth was reaped (Matt. 13:30)." Here the last judgment is compared to the grain harvest (Isa. 27:12–13; Jer. 51:33; Hos. 6:11; Joel 3:13a; 4 Ezra 4:26–40; 2 Bar. 70:2; Matt. 13:24–30, 36–43).

The sixth and seventh angels, 14:17–20.

In the second subunit, the last judgment is compared to the harvest of grapes (vv. 17–20; cf. Joel 3:13; Isa. 63:2–6). Another angel (= the sixth in the series) comes out of the temple in heaven carrying a sharp sickle. Then yet another angel (= the seventh in the series) comes from the altar and calls to the one with the sickle: "Put in your sickle, and gather the clusters of the vine on earth, for its grapes are ripe." So the sixth angel swung his sickle and gathered the vintage of the earth, "and threw it into the great wine press of the wrath of God; and the wine press was trodden outside the city, and blood flowed from the wine press, as high as a horse's bridle, for about two hundred miles" (cf. 1 Enoch 100:1–3, which says that at the final battle streams will flow with the blood of the slain so deep that the horses will walk up to the breast in the blood of sinners and the chariots shall be submerged to their height). It will be a terrible thing to behold (cf. 6 Ezra 15:35–36).

In the Apocalypse of John the last judgment is spoken of in terms of three primary images. First, in 6:12–17 and 16:17–21 it is described as a theophany (cf. 4 Ezra 7:38–42; 9:3–5). In the first, the reader does not witness the judgment but hears about it from those who are its witnesses. The agents of judgment in this context are God and the Lamb. In the second, the readers are allowed to witness the scene briefly. The agent of judgment is God.

Second, in 14:14–20 the last judgment is depicted as a world harvest (4 Ezra 4:29–30; Matt. 13:30). Here the reader witnesses the harvest but only in the very briefest of terms. The agents of judgment in this context are angels.

Third, in 20:11–15 the final judgment is cast as a courtroom/throne-room drama (Dan. 7:9–10; 1 Enoch 25:3; 90:20; Testament of Abraham 11:4; 12:4; T. Levi 5:1; 2 Cor. 5:10). Again the readers are allowed to witness the scene but only in its broad strokes. Here the agent of judgment is God. Revelation attests to the reality of the last judgment but with language so varied that one cannot read it univocally (= non-analogically). Theologically, the last judgment functions to underscore the seriousness with which human responsibility is taken. It says that our choices have *ultimate* consequences.

It should be clear from the foregoing discussion that there is an over-lap between Revelation's speech about the wrath of God and judgment. Both involve God's resistance to evil in His creation. Both involve present (= within history) and future (= at the end of history) dimensions. The last judgment corresponds with the revelation of wrath at the last day. Fur-thermore, judgment and wrath within history both correspond to the trib-ulation as it is experienced by non-believers. In this sense, there is an overlap among the concepts of wrath, judgment, and tribulation as they are used in Revelation.

If vision three (11:19–13:18) clarified Rome's role in the sufferings of Christians, vision four (14:1–20) makes crystal clear the price not only Rome but also those who sympathize with Rome will pay. Judgment, both within and at the end of history, is their reward. This is the gospel pro-claimed by angelic means in Revelation 14. It will be reinforced in vision five (15:1–16:21) that follows.

THE SEVEN PLAGUES OF WRATH
REVELATION 15:1–16:21

After the opening section of the prophet's call and his seven letters to the churches of Asia (1:9–3:22), there follow seven visions of the end times (4:1–8:1; 8:2–11:18; 11:19–13:18; 14:1–20; 15:1–16:21; 17:1–19:5; 19:6–22:5). These visions are arranged in two groups of three visions each, followed by a final seventh one. The first two visions (4:1–8:1; 8:2–11:18) in the first group cover basically the same material. Focus is on the tribula-tion (= the great period of suffering that immediately precedes the parou-sia), especially as it impacts Christians. The third vision in that group functions to clarify in concrete terms the nature of the tribulation as Chris-tians experience it. Christians' sufferings in the tribulation are caused by Roman imperial power because Christians will not worship in the emperor cult. Behind Rome's hostility lies the power and wrath of the great red dragon, Satan.

In group two, the first two visions (14:1–20; 15:1–16:21) also cover basically the same territory. Focus is on judgment both within history (= the tribulation) and at the end of history (= the last judgment), especially as it impacts non-Christians and faithless Christians. The third vision of group two (17:1–19:5) functions analogously to the third vision in group one. It makes clear in concrete terms who it is that is the object of judg-ment within and at the end of history and why it is so. At this point in the commentary, we have finished with the first vision in group two (14:1–20) and are ready to begin a survey of the second (15:1–16:21). It is well to remember that its focus is on judgment, especially of the non-Christian world. Revelation 15:1–16:21 is a thought unit composed of two parts: an opening scene in heaven (15:1–16:1), which serves to give reassurance to the auditors of the Apocalypse, and the pouring out of the seven bowls of God's wrath (16:2–21). Each must be examined in order.

Revelation 15:1–16:1 = Opening Scene in Heaven

The opening scene in heaven falls into an ABA' pattern.

A 15:1—The seven angels with the seven plagues
   B 15:2–4—Proleptic vision of the conquerors in heaven
A' 15:5–16:1—The seven angels with the seven plagues

Each part needs attention.

In 15:1, part A, John sees seven angels with seven plagues "which are the last, for with them the wrath of God is ended." The plagues are expressions of God's wrath (= His resistance to evil in His creation).

In 15:2–4, part B, the prophet sees in heaven what appears to be a sea of glass (= the location is before the throne, 4:6). Beside the sea stand those who have conquered the beast with its image and the number of its name. In Revelation, "to conquer" means to remain faithful to God/Christ even unto death (= not to assimilate to Roman imperial culture; 2:7, 11, 17, 26; 3:5, 12, 21). These conquerors have harps in their hands and are singing the song of Moses (= a song to celebrate God's deliverance of His people, Ex. 15:1; Deut. 32; Philo, *On the Contemplative Life* 85–88) and the Lamb (= the new song, 5:9, celebrating God's new deliverance through the Lamb):

> Great and wonderful are Thy deeds, O Lord God the Almighty!
> Just and true are Thy ways, O King of the ages!
> Who shall not fear and glorify Thy name, O Lord?
>   For Thou alone art holy.
> All nations shall come and worship Thee,
>   For Thy judgments have been revealed (cf. Ps. 86:9–10).

In 15:5–16:1, part A', attention returns to the seven angels and the seven plagues. Out of the heavenly temple (8:3–5) come seven angels with seven plagues. One of the four living creatures (4:6b–8; 5:14) gives the seven angels seven golden bowls full of the wrath of God. The temple is then filled with smoke (= a sign of the divine presence) from the glory of God and from His power (1 Kings 8:10; Isa. 6:4; Ezek. 44:4) so that no one can even enter. What is about to transpire originates in the presence of God. That it follows the worship of the conquerors implies (as in 8:2–5) that what follows flows from Christian worship. Again, from John's point of view, the most significant thing Christians can do to change the world is to worship God and to pray. Why? It is because just and lasting change in the world ultimately is God's doing.

A comparison of apocalyptic and modern views about evil casts light on John of Patmos's contention. To understand the ancient Jewish apocalyptic view, a development must be traced from prophecy. In Old Testament prophecy evil is regarded as a problem that can be corrected through proper discipline administered by God. Take Jeremiah, for example. This prophet's message can be summarized in essentially three points.

A word about the present: Israel has sinned.

A word of judgment: Because Israel has sinned, Yahweh will send judgment upon her. This judgment takes a this-worldly form. It takes the form of a foreign nation coming, making war against Judah, conquering Judah, and taking her king and chief citizens away into Babylonian exile.

A word about the future: After seventy years, those who are alive when the return from exile takes place will be allowed to return to their own land and live under their own king in peace and prosperity. Here, in Jeremiah, evil is understood to be like a child's misdirection that can be corrected by proper judgment/discipline. This is an optimistic view of evil.

When the pious Jews returned from Babylonian exile as was promised, the situation was no better than before the exile. In fact, a reading of Haggai, Zechariah, and Malachi indicates it may have been worse. Sin was everywhere prevalent. Consider, however, that only the righteous Jews had returned. Those who were interested only in business stayed behind in Babylon. The evil in postexilic Judaism, therefore, came from the righteous remnant. This new realism about evil comes to expression in the postexilic editing of the Pentateuch. In the Noah stories (Gen. 6–9), God determines to rid the world of human unrighteousness. He takes only the righteous Noah and his family, seals them in an ark, and saves them from the flood. With all others destroyed, the flood recedes and out comes the righteous Noah. What does he do? He and his son Ham both sin (9:20–27). The point? Good and evil are so intertwined within even the righteous that they cannot be separated within history (cf. Matt. 13:24–30). Preexilic prophetic optimism has been replaced by postexilic realism.

During the Seleucid rule of the Jews in the second century B.C., Antiochus Epiphanes structured life in such a way that to be a faithful Jew meant economic disaster and possible death; to be faithless to the Law enabled economic success and untroubled life. Early Jewish apocalyptic thinkers reflect this state of affairs. Their message also has three points.

A word about the present: The present evil age is dominated by Satan, infected by sin, and ruled by suffering and death.

A word about judgment: Because of the evil in creation, judgment is coming. Because evil is so deep-seated and radical, however, it cannot be dealt with by a this-worldly judgment. Rather, judgment takes the form of the end of the world. God wipes the slate clean. He will not allow evil to have immortality, so He brings the whole historical process to an end. Judgment in apocalyptic takes the form of the last judgment, the end of the world.

A word about the future: God will create new heavens and a new earth in which righteousness dwells. Who will dwell within this new world? Only those whom He raises from the dead. Here is a pessimistic view of evil. Evil is deep-seated and radical. It is a mystery that only God can resolve in any ultimate way.

In the modern West, evil is understood as a problem, a rock in the road that can be removed by human insight and resources. When a problem is sensed, one needs to work out a plan via human reason and appropriate the necessary human resources to solve it. After this problem is solved, there is an incremental betterment in human life. When the next problem arises, one should do the same thing. The result will be a history of gradually improving human life, thanks to human reason and human resources. In such a scheme, prayer is deemed a waste of time. Only human effort in the world makes a difference.

An apocalyptic thinker would consider this an incredibly naive view of the world. He would point out that because evil is so deep-seated and radical, every human solution to a problem contains within it the seeds of even more problems. The human solution is so fraught with evil that the very solution to evil itself breeds evil. Here evil is a mystery that only God can ultimately resolve. In such a frame of reference, prayer seems like the most important thing the people of God can do for the world. Evil is rampant; God needs to act; so pray!

Following the conquerors' worship in heaven, the stage is set for the seven angels to act. Although equipped (v. 7), they do not act until commanded: "Then I heard a loud voice from the temple telling the seven angels, 'Go and pour out on the earth the seven bowls of the wrath of God'" (16:1). Now they can go.

Revelation 16:2–21 = The Seven Bowls of God's Wrath

According to Lev. 26:21, the Lord promises to bring more plagues (= more than those of Egypt) upon humans when they walk contrary to His will. So it is here. The plagues mentioned in Lev. 26:14–39 (disease, famine, wild beasts, sword, pestilence) are not precisely those of Revelation 16, however. Nor are the plagues of Revelation 16 exactly those of the plagues in Egypt, although there is some overlap. The overlap will be pointed out as each of the seven plagues is discussed. A remarkable correspondence does exist, however, between the contents and order of vision two, the seven trumpets (8:2–11:18), and vision five, the seven plagues (15:1–16:21).

The Seven Trumpets	The Seven Plagues
1. the earth (v. 7)	1. the earth (v. 2)
2. the sea (v. 9)	2. the sea (v. 3)
3. rivers and fountains (v. 10)	3. rivers and fountains (v. 4)
4. sun, moon, stars (v. 12)	4. sun (v. 8)
5. darkness, torture (vv. 2, 5)	5. darkness, anguish (v. 10)
6. the Euphrates (v. 14)	6. the Euphrates (v. 12)
7. loud voices in heaven (v. 15)	7. loud voice from throne (v. 17)

The vision of the seven plagues is hereby seen as repetition with variation. This vision goes over much the same territory as the earlier vision, but with a different focus. There it was on the tribulation, especially as it affected believers; here it is on judgment as it affects, especially, unbelievers. There it was only one-third of the world that was affected; here it is all of nature that is touched. Indeed, the seven plagues of Revelation 16 seem to be the working out of the Christian conviction expressed in 2 Thess. 1:6: "God deems it just to repay with affliction those who afflict you." The image is that of Psalm 79:6: "Pour out Thy anger on the nations that do not know Thee, and on the kingdoms that do not call on Thy name."

The first bowl, 15:2.

The first plague comes in v. 2: "The first angel went and poured his bowl upon the earth, and foul and evil sores (Ex. 9:8–12, sixth plague of the Egyptian series) came upon the men who bore the mark of the beast and worshiped its image." The plague is upon those who have assimilated to Roman imperial culture and its idolatrous religion.

The second bowl, 15:3.

The second plague comes in v. 3: "The second angel poured his bowl into the sea, and it became like the blood of a dead man (Ex. 7:14–20, first plague of the Egyptian series), and every living thing died that was in the sea." This plague is tied to the next one.

The third bowl, 15:4–7.

The third plague comes in vv. 4–7: "The third angel poured his bowl into the rivers and fountains of water, and they became blood (Ex. 7:14–20, first plague of the Egyptian series; Ps. 78:44)." Whereas the second plague is directed to salt water, the third is aimed at fresh water.

The interlude, 15:5–7.

Following the third plague there is an interlude of two voices. (Remember a similar interlude of two voices in 14:13?) First, the third plague is announced by the angel of water to be a punishment that fits the crime (Wisdom of Solomon 11:16, "one is punished by the very things by which he sins"):

> Just art Thou in these Thy judgments . . . O Holy One.
> For men have shed the blood of saints and prophets,
> and Thou hast given them blood to drink. It is their due!

Second, the altar in heaven gives a responding cry:

> Yea, Lord God the Almighty, true and just are Thy judgments!

A dual witness underscores the truth of the assertion (cf. Ps. 119:137).

The fourth bowl, 15:8–9.

The fourth plague comes in vv. 8–9: "The fourth angel poured his bowl on the sun, and it was allowed to scorch men with fire; men were scorched by the fierce heat, and they cursed the name of God who had power over these plagues, and they did not repent and give Him glory."

Although the seven bowls of wrath do not correspond exactly to the plagues in Egypt, there is enough correspondence between the two series to evoke the Exodus events in the minds of the auditors of Revelation 16. In so doing, John causes his hearers to recollect that the purpose of the Egyptian plagues was to cause the repentance of Pharoah. In each case, however, Pharoah's heart was hardened and he did not repent (Ex. 7:22; 8:15, 19, 32; 9:7, 12, 34; 10:1, 20, 27; 11:10; 14:4, 8). So it is with the tribulation/judgment symbolized in the series of the seven bowls of God's wrath. Alas, the result is the same as in the case of Pharoah: "They did not repent and give Him glory" (v. 9).

The fifth bowl, 15:10–11.

The fifth plague comes in vv. 10–11: "The fifth angel poured his bowl on the throne of the beast, and its kingdom was in darkness (Ex. 10:21–29, ninth plague of the Egyptian series); men gnawed their tongues in anguish and cursed the God of heaven for their pain and sores, and did not repent of their deeds." The beast, of course, is the first beast of Rev. 13:1–8, Roman imperial power symbolized by its reigning emperor. Normally, the Apocalypse reserves "throne" for God (1:4; 3:21; 4:2, 3, 4, 5, 6, 9; 5:1, 6, 7, 11, 13, 16; 7:9, 10, 11, 15, 17; 8:3; 12:5; 14:3, 5; 16:17; 19:4, 5; 20:11;

21:5; 22:1, 3). Here, however, there is a reference to the throne (= the power, authority) of the beast. From 13:2 we know its source: "And to it (= the beast from the sea) the dragon gave his power and his throne and great authority." Darkness comes upon Roman authority and power (Wisdom of Solomon 17). Did humans repent of their sin? No. They "did not repent of their deeds." In vision five, as at the Exodus, the plagues do not bring repentance; rather, they reveal the true nature of the followers of the beast. They are confirmed in their sin.

The sixth bowl, 15:12–16.

The sixth plague comes in vv. 12–16: "The sixth angel poured his bowl on the great river Euphrates, and its water was dried up, to prepare the way for the kings from the east." Several streams of thought flow into this statement. First, there is the notion that there will be a great, final battle between God and the forces of evil in the end times (20:7–10). Second, here the Nero legend crops up again. One version of that legend said that Nero fled from Rome to the Parthians and that from thence he would return either to destroy Rome or to persecute God's people or both. The Sib. Or. 4.115–124 puts it thus:

> An evil storm of war will also come upon Jerusalem from Italy, and it will sack the great Temple of God. . . . Then a great king will flee from Italy like a runaway slave unseen and unheard over the channel of the Euphrates, when he dares to incur a maternal curse for repulsive murder . . . When he runs away, beyond the Parthian land, many will bloody the ground for the throne of Rome.

"Kings of the east" in v. 12 refers to the expectation, which was part of the Nero legend, that the Parthians would invade from beyond the Euphrates. Nero would be their leader. Their way is made easy by drying up of the river's waters. They can now cross on dry ground. The first prerequisite for the final battle has been made.

The second prerequisite is given in vv. 13–14: "I saw issuing from the mouth of the dragon and from the mouth of the beast and from the mouth of the false prophet, three foul spirits like frogs (Ex. 8:1–15, second plague of the Egyptian series); for they are demonic spirits, performing signs, who go abroad to the kings of the world, to assemble them for battle on the great day of God the Almighty." The first thing to notice here is that the dragon-first beast-second beast triumvirate of Revelation 12–13 has been transposed to dragon-beast-false prophet, as in 19:20 and 20:10. The second beast is the false prophet, the one who promotes emperor worship. False prophets are a stock item in apocalyptic thought (Matt. 7:15; 24:11, 24; Mark 13:22; Luke 6:26; 2 Peter 2:1; 1 John 4:1). Whereas early Christians believed that false prophets are always present among God's people

(2 Peter 2:1; Matt. 7:15), they believed also that such deceivers have a special role in the events of the end time: they will lead many astray; if possible, even the elect (Matt. 24:11, 24; Mark 13:22). This belief in the deceptive role of false prophets in the end time is focused in the Apocalypse of John on one false prophet who is associated with the beast and the dragon. The three make up a triumvirate of evil over against God, Christ, and the true prophet, John. Taken together, they symbolize the devil, godless government, and false religion.

The second item of note is that three demonic spirits come out of their mouths. That is, the three foul spirits like frogs symbolize some type of false, evil propaganda.[32] That they are demonic spirits fits ancient assumptions, Jewish and pagan. It states in 1 Enoch 53:3; 56:1 that demons punish the condemned. Plutarch, *On the Control of Anger* 9, tells us that execution of punishment is a task of demons.

Third, notice that this propaganda has a clearcut purpose. It is to gather the kings of the whole world for battle.

Fourth, consider the place at which they gather: "called in Hebrew Armageddon" (v. 16). Literally, this means "mountain of Mageddon." There is no such place in Palestinian geography. Perhaps Mageddon means Megiddo, a fortress city in northern Israel where some major battles were fought in antiquity (Judg. 4:4–5:31; 2 Kings 23:28–29). There is, however, no mountain at Megiddo, which is located on a plain (cf. Judg. 5:19; 2 Chron. 35:22). This must surely mean that Armageddon does not refer to a geographical site on a map. It is rather the location in apocalyptic mythology for the last eschatological battle involving the kings of the earth under the leadership of the devil.

In the midst of the sixth plague there is a word from the risen Christ with a warning and a beatitude (v. 15; other beatitudes in Revelation include 1:3; 3:3; 14:13; 19:9; 20:6; and 22:14, 17):

> Lo, I am coming like a thief!
> Blessed is he who is awake, keeping his garments
> that he may not go naked and be seen exposed! (3:2a, 3b).

The warning sounds very similar to the sayings found in Matt. 24:42–44// Mark 13:35–37//Luke 12:35–40 and to a similar one in Matt. 25:13 at the end of the parable of the ten virgins who were waiting for the bridegroom. Of these parallel passages, only Luke 12:35–40 combines the note of Christ's sudden appearance with congratulations to those who are prepared. This is one of a number of sayings of the risen Christ in Revelation that sound similar to logia found in the mouth of the pre-Easter Jesus in the Synoptics: 1:3 (Luke 11:28); 1:7 (Matt. 24:30); 2:7, 11, 17, 29; 3:6, 13, 22; 13:9 (Mark 4:9, 23; Matt. 11:15; 13:9; Luke 8:8; 14:35); 3:5c (Matt.

10:32; Luke 12:8); 3:20 (Luke 12:36–37); 3:21 (Luke 22:28–30); 13:10a, b (Matt. 26:52).[33] To auditors who have heard the gospels read in worship, these words in the Apocalypse have the effect of reinforcing the identity of the pre-Easter Jesus and the risen Christ.

The seventh bowl, 15:17–21.

The seventh bowl is poured out in 15:17–21: "The seventh angel poured his bowl into the air, and a loud voice came out of the temple, from the throne (= of God), saying, 'It is done!'" (*gegonen* = perfect tense, meaning, "it has been accomplished and remains so"). With the seventh bowl there is an announcement of the accomplishment of God's will upon the earth. What follows is a description of a theophany and its effects. The theophany (= manifestation of the divine presence) includes these elements:

> And there were flashes of lightning, voices, peals of thunder (11:19), and a great earthquake (6:12; 11:19) such as there had never been since men were on the earth . . . (v. 18). And every island fled away, and no mountains were to be found (6:14; 1 Enoch 6:12–14; Assumption of Moses 10:4) (v. 20); and great hailstones (11:19; Ex. 9:13–34, the seventh in the Egyptian series of plagues; hail was part of the arsenal of divine retribution, Josh. 10:11; Ezek. 38:18–22), heavy as a hundredweight, dropped on men from heaven (v. 21).

The effects of the theophany are given in v. 19:

> The great city (= Rome; 17:18) was split into three parts (= complete destruction), and the cities of the nations fell, and God remembered great Babylon (= Rome, 17:5, 9), to make her drain the cup of the fury of His wrath (14:10).

If the series of plagues began by specifying the objects of God's wrath (men who bore the mark of the beast and worshiped its image, vs. 2), it ends with ultimate judgment on Rome and her allies (v. 19). Although the plagues were designed to elicit repentance (16:9, 11), their effect has been simply to harden the hearts of the non-Christians who suffered: "Men cursed God for the plague of the hail, so fearful was that plague."

For those who recognize the principle of recapitulation at work in Revelation, it is clear that the series of eschatological woes in 16:1–21 is not a chronological continuation of the preceding series in 14:6–20. The two visions refer to the same period but from different perspectives. They involve repetition with variation. It is also important to understand that when Revelation's visions repeat with variation, they speak with the voices of multiple eschatological traditions. There is often diversity in details. For example, in 16:17–21 the consummation is due to God's direct activity: His proclamation (v. 17b) and theophany (vv. 18–21). In 14:14–20, however, the eschatological harvest is due to angels, not God directly. In 19:11–21, to which we will come soon, one part of the final victory is won by the Messiah, whereas in 20:9b it is due to God's direct intervention. This type of diversity teaches a reader of the Apocalypse not to expect of this type of language a precision that other types of discourse may provide. It would be a mistake to take chapters 14, 16, and 19, for example, as referring to three different events.

The overall message of Revelation's fifth vision (15:1–16:21) is quite clear: in heaven those who have conquered the beast sing the song of Moses and the Lamb, a vision offering reassurance to Christian auditors; and God's wrath is poured out on Rome and on those with the mark of the beast, but it does not elicit their repentance.

Two visions (14:1–20 and 15:1–16:21) in the second group of three in the Apocalypse of John have focused on the judgment that comes on the beast and its devotees both within and at the end of history. In the third vision of the second grouping (17:1–19:5) one is offered an explanation of the identity of the beast, its role in the sufferings of Christians, and the results, given in great detail, of its behavior. To this vision we now turn.

THE ROLE AND RESULTS OF IMPERIAL POWER
REVELATION 17:1–19:5

After the opening letters to the seven churches (2:1–3:22) Revelation comprises seven visions of the end times. These seven visions fall into two groups of three (group one = 4:1–8:1; 8:2–11:18; 11:19–13:18; group two = 14:1–20; 15:1–16:21; 17:1–19:5), followed by a final vision dealing with the consummation (19:6–22:5). The first group focuses on the tribulation as it affects Christians; the second group depicts the judgment upon the opponents of Christians and upon their sympathizers. In each of the two groups, the third vision functions to give clarity to the concrete circumstances dealt with in general terms by the preceding two visions. So in 11:19–13:18, Roman imperial power, rooted in the dragon's authority and wrath, is exposed as the persecutor of the Christians. In 17:1–19:5 the role of imperial power in the sufferings of Christians is exposed and the downfall of Rome, as a result, is promised. Like all seven visions, 17:1–19:5 begins with some type of heavenly scene that functions to give reassurance to the auditors of the Apocalypse (17:1–2). Like the third vision of the first group, the material that follows the initial heavenly vision falls into five, not seven, scenes. A survey of vision six is now in order.

This is a thought unit composed of two parts: an opening scene in heaven (17:1–2) and five scenes dealing with the judgment of the harlot of Babylon (17:3–19:5).

Revelation 17:1–2 = Opening Heavenly Vision

One of the seven angels who had poured out the seven bowls of wrath upon the earth (16:1–21) comes to the prophet, John, with a heavenly promise: "Come, I will show you the judgment of the great harlot who is seated upon many waters, with whom the kings of the earth have committed fornication, and with the wine of whose fornication the dwellers upon the earth have become drunk" (17:1b–2). Just as in the Old Testament pagan cities are sometimes called harlots (Isa. 23:16, Tyre; Nahum 3:4 Nineveh) to reflect their spiritual condition, so it is here (cf. 17:18, "the woman that you saw is the great city . . . "). Just as Jeremiah 51:13 speaks of Babylon as by/upon many waters, so here (17:5, "Babylon the great, mother of harlots"). Just as in the Old Testament faithlessness to God is sometimes described as fornication (Jer. 3:9; Ezek. 16:15–22; Hos. 4:15, 18), so here (17:2). The harlot spoken of here is a city that is faithless to God. The angel gives heaven's promise: Her judgment is coming! What follows in 17:3–19:5 is the fulfillment of this promise.

Revelation 17:3–19:5 = The Judgment of the Harlot

The judgment of the harlot falls into five scenes: 17:3–18; 18:1–3; 18:4–20; 18:21–24; and 19:1–5. Each must be examined in order.

The first scene, 17:3–18.

The first scene consists of two subunits: a vision (vv. 3–6) and an interpretation of the vision (vv. 7–18).

In vv. 3–6, there is a vision of the harlot. The angel carries the prophet away in the Spirit (= prophetic inspiration, 1:10; 4:12; 21:10) into a wilderness. There he sees "a woman sitting on a scarlet beast which was full of blasphemous names, and it had seven heads and ten horns." The woman was "arrayed in purple and scarlet, and bedecked with gold and jewels and pearls, holding in her hand a golden cup full of abominations and impurities of her fornication; and on her forehead was written a name of mystery: 'Babylon the great' . . . And I saw the woman, drunk with the blood of the saints and the blood of the martyrs of Jesus."

The woman's attire speaks of royalty and wealth. Her seat (on a beast with blasphemous names), her cup (full of defilement), her name (Baby-

lon = Rome, in 2 Esdras 3:1–2, 28–31; 2 Bar. 10:1–3; Sib. Or. 5.143, 159)
written on her forehead (Roman courtesans placed their names on their
foreheads, Juvenal 6.123), and her behavior (the cause of Christian martyrdoms) all attest her wickedness. Is it any wonder, then, that when the writer
saw her, he "marvelled greatly" (17:6b)? If the third vision of the first
group of three began with a woman (12:1–2) who turned out to be the
people of God, the third vision of the second group of three also begins
with a woman. She is not the people of God, however. Quite the opposite!
Who then is she?

The angel proceeds to interpret the vision to John in 17:7–18: "Why
marvel? I will tell you the mystery of the woman, and of the beast with
seven heads and ten horns that carries her."

The beast is first identified: "The beast that you saw was, and is not,
and is to ascend from the bottomless pit and go to perdition" (v. 8a). This
is yet another echo in Revelation of the Nero legend. One form of the
Nero legend held that Nero was alive and would return from Parthia (Sib.
Or. 4.119–24, 137–39; 8.70–72, 155–57). Another version held that Nero
had died but that he would return, the incarnation of Beliar/the devil, as
the Antichrist (Ascension of Isaiah 4:2–12). It is the latter version that is
assumed here. The beast, then, represents Roman imperial power symbolized by Nero returning from the pit of Hell: "As for the beast that was and
is not, it is an eighth but it belongs to the seven, and it goes to perdition" (v.
11). The beast belongs to a line of Roman kings, as its last representative. It
symbolizes the final emperor, the Antichrist.[34]

Jewish. In Jewish apocalyptic writings there is often found an evil individual who is to arise in the last days as an opponent of God. He is the end
tyrant. He tries to deceive God's people and to lead them astray; he persecutes them if they remain faithful to God. In Daniel 7–12, the end tyrant
is identified as Antiochus Epiphanes, the Seleucid ruler whose policies pro-
voked the Maccabean war. In 2 Bar. 36:5, he is the last Roman emperor (as
in Rev. 17:11). In 4 Ezra 11:40–46, he is the Roman Empire itself. In the
Testaments of the Twelve Patriarchs, the end tyrant is the embodiment of
Beliar (T. Issachar 6:1; T. Dan 5:10; T. Judah 25:3). In Sib. Or. 4.138–39,
he is Nero returning from Parthia.

Early Christian. In early Christian sources there is also found an expectation of a human opponent of God in the end time. His functions are
two: to deceive and to persecute. Mark 13:21–22 speaks about false Christs
who attempt to lead God's people astray. Second Thessalonians 2:3–4, 8–
12 talks about the man of lawlessness who represents Satan and uses
miracles to deceive. First John 2:18–19, 20–27; 4:3 and 2 John 7 speak

about many antichrists who have already come (= schismatics who deceive, denying the humanity of the church's savior). The Didache 16:4–5 speaks about the deceiver of the world who appears as the Son of God, doing miracles, committing iniquities, and causing some to fall away. The Apocalypse of Peter 2 refers to a deceiving Christ who performs miracles, seeking to turn believers away, and who, when rejected, martyrs them. The Greek Apocalypse of Ezra alludes to the "opponent" who comes up from Tartarus (3:15) and seeks to lead people astray. The Coptic Apocalypse of Elijah mentions a son of lawlessness, a king, who performs miracles and causes Christian martyrdoms. Hippolytus, *Treatise on Christ and Antichrist* 49, 57, refers to the Antichrist as a king, a vessel of Satan, a deceiver, and a persecutor.

Revelation. In Revelation 17 the beast that carries the woman is the Antichrist. He is the final king who comes from the underworld. The way he is described sets him over against Christ. If Christ is the one "who was and is and is to come" (Rev. 4:8b), the beast is he who "was and is not and is to come" (17:8b). The "dwellers on the earth whose names have not been written in the book of life from the foundation of the world, will marvel to behold the beast, because it was and is not and is to come" (v. 8b). The beast, then, is Roman imperial power embodied in its last emperor who happens to fulfill certain expectations about Nero's return.

What about the seven heads on the beast? "This calls for a mind with wisdom: the seven heads are seven mountains on which the woman is seated" (v. 9). It was widely known that Rome was the city on seven hills (Virgil, *Aeneid* 6.782; Martial 4.64). The seven heads, then, are geographically interpreted in v. 9. In v. 10, however, an additional interpretation is given: "They are also seven kings, five of whom have fallen, one is, the other has not yet come, and when he comes he must remain only a little while." This statement has been a battleground for scholars arguing over the date of Revelation. How do its kings fit with a list of Roman emperors? A list of emperors and their dates looks like this.

Julius Caesar	died 44 B.C.
Augustus	31 B.C.–A.D. 14
Tiberius	A.D. 14–37
Caligula	A.D. 37–41
Claudius	A.D. 41–54
Nero	A.D. 54–68
Galba	A.D. 68–69
Otho	A.D. 69
Vitellius	A.D. 69

Vespasian	A.D. 69–79
Titus	A.D. 79–81
Domitian	A.D. 81–96
Nerva	A.D. 96–98
Trajan	A.D. 98–117

Revelation 17:10 says five have fallen, one is, and the other is yet to come. Two problems present themselves. First, should we begin with Julius Caesar (as Josephus, 4 Ezra, and Suetonius do) or with Augustus (as Tacitus does)? Second, should we include Galba, Otho, and Vitellius, or exclude them (as Suetonius, *Vespasian* 1, does) from the list? Depending upon which of the two alternatives one chooses, the correlation varies. If one starts with Julius Caesar and includes Galba, Otho, and Vitellius, then the five who have fallen go through Claudius; the one who is is Nero; and the one yet to come is Galba. If one starts with Julius and excludes Galba, Otho, and Vitellius, then the one yet to come is Vespasian. If one starts with Augustus and includes Galba, Otho, and Vitellius, then the five who have fallen go through Nero; the one who is is Galba; and the one to come is Otho. If one starts with Augustus and excludes Galba, Otho, and Vitellius, then the one who is is Vespasian and the one to come is Titus. He is to remain only a little while, and then comes the eighth, Domitian. If this all seems confusing and incapable of solution, it is because it is so.

The fact is, this list of kings seems very much like the conventional apocalyptic practice of numbering periods of world history (2 Esd. 14:11 divides history into twelve parts, of which nine and a half have already passed; 1 Enoch 93 divides history into ten periods, seven of which are past). In this light, Martin Kiddle offers wise words about the seven kings. He says:

> those who seek in the reference to seven kings a list of seven individual monarchs must admit that the text is enigmatic beyond hope. . . . the number seven has here its symbolical force—as always in Revelation. It is used to convey the complete number of the emperors—just as seven churches represent the complete number of Christian communities; just as the . . . plagues are neatly arranged in series of seven, to indicate that they will be complete.[35]

That five have fallen means the line is near its end. The seven heads of the beast are, therefore, both the geographical site of the city of Rome and the complete line of Roman emperors (= Roman imperial power).

What about the ten horns on the beast? They are ten kings who will "receive authority as kings for one hour (= a very brief time), together with the beast. These are of one mind and give over their power and authority to the beast" (v. 12). The Antichrist will have human allies. The functions of the ten kings are two. First, they will make war on the Lamb, but unsuccessfully. The Lamb will conquer them (v. 14; cf. 19:11–21). Second, they, together with the beast, will destroy the woman. "They will make her desolate and naked, and devour her flesh and burn her up with fire, for God has put it into their hearts to carry out his purpose by being of one mind and giving over their royal power to the beast, until the words of God (= the promise of the judgment of the harlot, 17:1–2) shall be fulfilled" (vv. 16b–17). And who is the woman who will be destroyed? "And the woman that you saw is the great city (= Rome), which has dominion over the kings of the earth" (v. 18).

Only the waters on which the woman is seated remain uninterpreted. The angel says: "The waters . . . where the harlot is seated are peoples and multitudes and nations and tongues" (v. 15). Rome rules a multitude of peoples of all kinds.

John has been shown a vision of a woman sitting on a beast. The angel has interpreted the vision to him. The woman is Rome. The beast is both Rome's geographical location and the imperial power on which she depends. The last of her kings, the Antichrist, will join forces with a full band of other rulers in the end time to fight unsuccessfully against the Lamb, but successfully against the city. The city that is drunk with the blood of Christian martyrs (17:6) will be destroyed by the very institution on which she depends for survival: the power of the emperors. The identity of the players having been established in 17:3–18, the vision now turns in 18:1–19:5 to the collapse of the antichristian world order, the judgment of the harlot.

The second scene, 18:1–3.

The second scene in vision six comes in 18:1–3. It is an angelic announcement of Babylon's doom. Another angel comes down from heaven, "having great authority" (v. 1). He cries:

> Fallen, fallen is Babylon the great! [Isa. 21:9]
> It has become a dwelling place of demons,
> a haunt of every foul spirit,
> a haunt for every foul and hateful bird [Isa. 34:13–15];
> *for* all nations have drunk the wine of her impure passion,
> and the kings of the earth have committed fornication with her,
> and the merchants of the earth have grown rich with the wealth of her
>   wantonness (Rev. 18:2b–3).

It is easy to see why the world was taken with Rome. An inscription at Halicarnassus celebrates the Emperor Augustus as savior of the whole human race.

> Land and sea have peace, the cities flourish under a good legal system, in harmony and with an abundance of food, there is an abundance of all good things,

people are filled with happy hopes for the future and with delight at the present.[36]

From John's perspective, these benefits are not what they seem. They are the favors of a prostitute, bought with a high price. Those who made money off Rome, entered into her idolatry. The temptation was great because the potential for wealth was enormous. Aelius Aristides says of Rome:

> So many merchant ships arrive here, conveying every kind of goods from every people every hour and every day, so so that the city is like a factory common to the whole earth. . . . So everything comes together here, trade, seafaring, farming, the scouring of the mines, all crafts that exist or have existed, all that is produced and grown. Whatever one does not see here is not a thing which has existed or exists.[37]

The angelic proclamation, however, is that Babylon (= Rome) has fallen and become desolate. This is because she involved others—nations, kings, and merchants—in her idolatry.

The third scene, 18:4–20.

In 18:4–20, the third scene, John hears yet another voice from heaven. The organization of this section is complex. It is held together by an inclusion: vv. 4–5 and 20, which are exhortations to God's people. Verses 4–5 say, "Come out of her, my people (Jer. 51:45; 2 Cor. 6:17; 1 Peter 4:3–5), lest you take part in her sins, lest you share in her plagues; for her sins are heaped high as heaven, and God has remembered her iniquities." Christians are exhorted to separate themselves spiritually from Roman imperial society, which is doomed. Many of John's auditors are among the affluent, the self-satisfied, and the compromising. For such, the prophet voices the peril of their situation as well.

Verse 20 says, "Rejoice over her, O heaven, O saints and apostles and prophets, for God has given judgment for you against her!" (Jer. 51:48; Rev. 6:9–11). Christians are exhorted to rejoice because God has answered their prayers.

Between the inclusion, made up of two exhortations, there are two sections, vv. 6–8 and vv. 9–19, both containing subunits. The first has two; the second has three.

The first exhortation in vv. 6–8 consists of a prayer (vv. 6–7a) and a response to the prayer (vv. 7b–8), joined by the keyword "mourning." The prayer asks for judgment upon Rome (cf. Ps. 137:8).

> Render to her as she herself has rendered,
> and repay her double for her deeds;
> mix a double draught for her in the cup she mixed.

> As she glorified herself and played the wanton,
> so give her a like measure of torment and *mourning* (Rev. 18:6–7a).

The answer comes as a prophetic oracle (cf. Isa. 47:8–9):

> Since in her heart she says, "A queen I sit,
> I am no widow, *mourning* I shall never see,"
> So shall her plagues come in a single day,
> pestilence and *mourning* and famine,
> and she shall be burned with fire;
> for mighty is the Lord God who judges her (Rev. 18:7b–8).

If in Rev. 6:9–11 the martyrs who prayed for vindication were told to wait a little longer, now the petitions of God's people are answered swiftly. Vindication is coming (Luke 18:1–7); Rome will be judged.

The second exhortation in vv. 9–19 consists of three dirges (cf. Isa. 13, 21, 34, 47; Jer. 25, 50–51; Ezek. 26–28; Nahum 3), each with a similar surface structure: the speaker is introduced, the dirge is given, and the suddenness of the fall is mentioned.

Verses 9–10 constitute the first funeral lament. The speakers are "the kings of the earth who committed fornication and were wanton with her." They "weep and wail over her when they see the smoke of her burning" (v. 9), saying

> "Alas! alas! thou great city,
> thou mighty city, Babylon!
> In one hour has thy judgment come" (v. 10).

Verses 11–17a make up the second lament. The speakers are the merchants of the earth who gained wealth from her (v. 15). They will weep because there is no longer anyone to buy their wares (v. 11). They will mourn aloud, saying

> "Alas, alas, for the great city
> that was clothed in fine linen, in purple and scarlet,
> bedecked with gold, with jewels, and with pearls!
> In one hour all this wealth has been laid waste" (vv. 16–17).

Verses 17b–19 comprise the third dirge. The speakers are all shipmasters and seafaring men, sailors and all those whose trade is on the sea. They weep and mourn, crying

> "Alas, alas for the great city
> where all who had ships at sea grew rich by her wealth!
> In one hour she has been laid waste" (v. 19b).

Scene three (18:4–20) has announced Babylon's (= Rome's) demise and has exhorted Christians both to be spiritually separate so as to avoid sharing her fate and to rejoice because God has vindicated them.

The fourth scene, 18:21–24.

Verses 21–24 consist of a doom song introduced by a symbolic action (cf. Jer. 51:63–64):

> Then a mighty angel took up a stone like a great millstone and threw it into the sea, saying,
>
> "So shall Babylon the great city be thrown down with violence, and shall be found no more . . . " (v. 21).

Why has this judgment come upon the great city? Two reasons are given. First, "for . . . all nations were deceived by thy sorcery" (v. 23c). This echoes Rev. 18:3, where Babylon's fall is due to her enlisting others in her idolatry. The harlot has seduced the world. Second, "in her was found the blood of prophets and of saints, and of all who have been slain on earth" (v. 24). This echoes Rev. 17:6, where the woman is drunk with the blood of the saints and the martyrs of Jesus and Rev. 18:20 where God's people are exhorted to rejoice at Babylon's fall because "God has given judgment for you against her." The sins of the great city are primarily two: idolatry, including enlistment of others in it, and persecution of the saints. For these sins her judgment has come.

The fifth scene, 19:1–5.

In 19:1–5 the final scene of vision six is given: "After this I heard what seemed to be the loud voice of a great multitude in heaven." Its three parts are held together by "Hallelujah" (= praise Yahweh) in vv. 1, 3, and 4. The first cry is this:

> "Hallelujah! Salvation and glory and power belong to our God, for His judgments are true and just;
> He has judged the great harlot who corrupted the earth . . .
> and He has avenged on her the blood of His servants" (Rev. 19:1b–2).

God is praised in a hymn of vindication, in response to the exhortation in Rev. 18:20 ("Rejoice over her, O heaven, O saints and apostles and prophets, for God has given judgment for you against her"). He is praised because the promise of 17:1–2 ("Come, I will show you the judgment of the great harlot") has been fulfilled. Judgment has come upon her because she has shed the blood of God's servants.

Although at the time Revelation was written, only one Christian martyr was known among the seven churches in the province of Asia (2:13, "Antipas my witness, my faithful one, who was killed among you"), the seven visions of the end times imply that many more (6:9–11; 7:14; 11:7–10; 13:15; 17:6; 18:24) are coming during the tribulation. Behind these martyrdoms is Rome (13:15; 17:6; 18:24) and ultimately the power of the dragon (11:7; 12:17).

Martyrdom was a matter about which Jews had knowledge. In 2 Maccabees, for example, one hears about both the aged Eleazar's death (6:28) and the deaths of the seven brothers (chap. 7). Their martyrdoms were seen as due to their obedience to the Law and as having expiatory benefits for Israel as a whole (cf. also 4 Maccabees 5–7, 8–13).

Some early Christians saw Jesus' death as a martyrdom, the prototype of later Christian martyrdoms. For example, in Luke-Acts Jesus is the first Christian martyr and Stephen his first follower in martyrdom (Acts 22:20, "the blood of Stephen thy witness was shed").

Revelation is very much a part of this trend. In the Apocalypse, Jesus is the proto-martyr. He is the faithful *martus* (= witness, martyr; cf. 1 Tim. 6:13), the firstborn from the dead, who has freed us by his blood (1:5; 3:14; cf. 2 Macc. 7:37–38; 4 Macc. 6:28–29). Faithful Christians also share his death (2:13; 11:3, 7; 17:6; 18:24) when necessary. Martyrdom is the ultimate resistance to the demand for assimilation to Roman imperial culture.[38]

The second cry repeats the refrain: "Hallelujah! The smoke from her goes up for ever and ever" (Rev. 19:3). The third cry comes not from the saints who have been vindicated but from the high angels around the throne: "And the twenty-four elders and the four living creatures fell down and worshiped God who is seated on the throne, saying, 'Amen [= so let it be] Hallelujah!'" (Rev. 19:4). Angels join the saints in praising the God who has delivered His people. This is something that is right and appropriate, as a voice from the throne indicates: "And from the throne came a voice, crying, 'Praise our God, all you his servants, you who fear Him, small and great'" (v. 5). If 17:1–2 begins with a promise of God's judgment of the harlot, and if 17:3–18:24 depicts the fulfillment of the promise, 19:1–5 presents the praise of God's people and the heavenly hosts closest to God for His fulfillment of His promise. The train of thought runs from promise to fulfillment to praise.

So far in the Apocalypse of John there have been three women mentioned; in vision seven (19:6–22:5) there will be a fourth. In Israel, given their social organization, women were described either as faithful wife or as harlot. These two dominant images are used in the Old Testament of Israel's relation to God: as faithful wife (Isa. 54:5; 62:5; Ezek. 16:8–14; Hos. 2:19–20) and as unfaithful wife (Jer. 3:20; Ezek. 16:15–22; Hosea 3). Women are portrayed in Revelation in terms of this Old Testament background.[39] Of the four women mentioned in Revelation, two are faithful to God, two are unfaithful.

The first woman mentioned is Jezebel (Rev. 2:20). She is a prophetess, preaching accommodation to pagan culture. She is attacked not because of her gender but because of her heresy.[40]

The second is the woman of Revelation 12 who gives birth to the Messiah, who endures the hostility of the dragon but is preserved by God's providence and protection. Here the woman is the people of God from whom Jesus and Christians come. This woman is regarded positively not because she is a woman but because she is in line with John's Christian presuppositions.

The third woman is the harlot of Revelation 17–18 who is drunk with the blood of saints. She represents Roman imperial culture opposed to Christ. Here Rome is not an unfaithful wife, since no original marriage relationship ever existed. Instead, she is a harlot, in part because she has seduced the world. Again, this woman is condemned and judged not because of her gender but because she is anti-Christian.

The fourth woman mentioned in Revelation is the bride of Christ the church, who is finally wed to Christ for all eternity (Revelation 19–21). She is treated positively not because of her gender but because of her relationship to Jesus. The fact of the matter is that no one, neither male nor female, is treated either positively or negatively in Revelation because of his or her gender. As in the rest of the New Testament, one's rating of approval or disapproval is determined by one's relationship to God/Christ/ the Holy Spirit or to the church.

With the four images of women in the Apocalypse, John offers his auditors a choice: either to persevere and await the bridegroom or to fall away and commit apostasy. When he treats women, as with his treatment of anything else, the issue for the prophet of Patmos is whether or not Christians are going to assimilate to Roman imperial culture. Anything or anyone that tends to assimilation is regarded negatively; anything or anyone who resists assimilation is regarded positively. The Apocalypse is dealing with a religious issue (First-Commandment faithfulness), not with sociology (men's and women's roles). The first is argued; the second is assumed (as part of the scandal of particularity) in order to communicate with people who, like us, were culturally conditioned.[41]

The first group of three visions focused on the tribulation experienced by Christians, suffering at the hands of Roman imperial power. The second group of three visions focused on the judgment coming on Rome because of idolatry and Rome's role in the persecution of Christians. What is left is vision seven, a vivid picture of the consummation of all things (19:6–22:5). To Revelation's grand finale we now turn.

THE CONSUMMATION
REVELATION 19:6–22:5

The overall surface structure of Revelation is relatively simple. There are first of all seven letters to seven churches in the province of Asia (2:1–3:22). These are followed by seven visions of the end times (4:1–8:1; 8:2–11:18; 11:19–13:18; 14:1–20; 15:1–16:21; 17:1–19:5; 19:6–22:5), each of which begins with a scene in heaven. The seven visions fall into two groups of three each, followed by a seventh. The first group of three focuses on the tribulation, especially as it impacts believers. The second group of three concentrates on the judgment that is coming on Rome and her allies. The seventh and final vision brings the shift of the ages to its completion. In 19:6–22:5 there is a grand vision of the consummation of all things. This thought unit, like the preceding six, is composed of two parts: 19:6–10, an opening scene in heaven, and 19:11–22:5, the consummation depicted by means of seven scenes. These two parts of the seventh vision need careful attention.

19:6–10 = Opening Scene in Heaven

The opening scene in heaven consists of an audition (vv. 6–8) and an angelic instruction (vv. 9–10).

John hears what seems to be the voice of a great multitude, crying:

"Hallelujah! For the Lord our God the Almighty reigns.
[Remember Rev. 11:15, 17?]
Let us rejoice and exult and give him the glory,
for the marriage of the Lamb has come,
and his Bride has made herself ready;
it was granted her to be clothed with fine linen" [Rev. 3:5, 18] . . .
for the fine linen is the righteous deeds of the saints.

In heaven a great multitude praise God because His reign is actualized and the marriage of the Lamb has come. Revelation uses various pictures for the New Age: heavenly worship (11:15–18; 14:1–5; 19:1–5; 19:6–7); the appearing of a new Jerusalem (21:2, 10–27); the regaining of paradise (22:1–5); and a wedding of the Messiah and the people of God (19:7; 21:2, 9). The last of these metaphors derives from the early Christian treatment of Christ as a bridegroom (Mark 2:19–20; Matt. 25:1–12; John 3:29; Eph. 5:32) and of the church as a bride (2 Cor. 11:2; Eph 5:27). Here amidst heavenly worship, an announcement is made that the evidence that God reigns is that the marriage of the Lamb has come. The bride is ready, clothed in righteous deeds (= deeds that reflect faithfulness to the covenant; cf. 3:5; 6:11; 7:9, 14; 16:15).[42]

An angelic instruction follows (vv. 9–10). It has three parts. First, there is a beatitude: "Blessed are (= Congratulations to) those who are invited to the marriage supper of the Lamb" (v. 9a; cf. Matt. 25:1–12). Here, in a complex metaphor, Christians are both the bride and the guests at the wedding feast. In effect, the beatitude asks the auditors whether or not they belong to the wedding party (as does the parable in Matt. 25:1–12). Second, there is a heavenly guarantee: "These are true words of God" (Rev. 19:9b). The promise that the end has come is a true word of God. The angel here guarantees it (cf. 10:1–7; 17:1–2; Mark 16:5–7). Again, the scene in heaven reassures the auditors. Third, when John falls down at the angel's feet to worship him, the angel resists him: "'You must not do that! I am a fellow servant with you and your brethren who hold the testimony of Jesus. Worship God.' For the testimony of Jesus is the spirit of prophecy" (v. 10). Remember, all the visions of Revelation are communicated through Jesus' angel (1:1; 22:6). Although mediators of revelation, angels remain creatures and are not to be worshiped (22:8–9). Angels and prophets alike are servants of God, and their function is to bear testimony to Jesus (John 15:26).[43]

What follows are seven scenes of the consummation, each introduced by the same refrain, *kai eidon/*"then I saw" (19:11, 17, 19; 20:1, 4, 11; 21:1). Each needs examination.

Revelation 19:11–22:5 = Seven Scenes of the Consummation

The first scene, 19:11–16.

"Then I saw (*kai eidon*) heaven opened, and behold a white horse!" There follows a description of the one who sits upon the white horse. His eyes are like a flame of fire (1:14; cf. Dan. 10:6). On his head are many diadems (= a sign of royalty, Isa. 62:3). He is clad in a robe dipped in blood (= a sign of a warrior, Isa. 9:5; 63:1–6). The name by which he is called is the Word of God (= the name of the divine warrior, Wisd. Sol. 18:15–16: "Thy all-powerful word leaped from heaven, from the royal throne, into the midst of the land that was doomed, a stern warrior carrying the sharp sword of authentic command"). He is accompanied by the armies of heaven (= the angelic hosts, 2 Enoch 17; T. Levi 3:3; Matt. 26:53). From his mouth issues a sharp sword with which to smite the nations (= a figure for judicial condemnation, Isa. 11:4; 1 Enoch 62:2; 4 Ezra 13:10; 2 Thess. 2:8). This is a picture of the warrior messiah found elsewhere in ancient Judaism and early Christianity (Psalms of Solomon 17:23–27, 31, 39; 2 Bar. 72; 4 Ezra 13:32–38; 1 Enoch 46:4–8; Palestinian Targum on Genesis 49:11: "How beautiful is the King Messiah . . . he girds his loins and goes out to battle . . . and he kills kings and rulers; he reddens the mountains with the blood of their slain; . . . his garments roll in the blood, and he is like one who presses grapes"[44]; 2 Thess. 1:7–8, 9–10; Matt. 25:41; Ascension of Isaiah 10:12; Sib. Or. 2:249–51). "On his robe and on his thigh he has a name inscribed, King of kings and Lord of lords" (= a characterization of God; cf. 17:14; Deut. 10:17; Dan. 2:47). The most natural way to read this is as a depiction of the parousia (= second coming) of Christ (cf. 1 Tim. 6:14; Heb. 9:28; 1 John 3:2; Apocalypse of Peter 1; Sib. Or. 2:241–44).

Scene two, 19:17–18.

The second scene begins *kai eidon*/"then I saw." John sees an angel standing in the sun (= brilliant appearance) who calls with a loud voice to all the birds that fly in mid-heaven: "Come, gather for the great supper of God, to eat the flesh of kings, the flesh of captains, the flesh of the mighty men, the flesh of horses and their riders, and the flesh of all men, both free and slave, both small and great."

The picture assumed here is that of a battlefield littered with dead bodies that have become food for vultures and other birds of carrion. This picture comes out of Ezek. 39:17–20, where it serves to describe God's victory over His enemies in the last great battle (16:12–16; 20:7–10; 2 Ezra 2; 2 Bar. 70–74; 1 QM 18). This final victory is gruesomely described as "the great supper of God." It is a very different meal from the marriage supper of the Lamb! There is no description of the actual warfare here, only an announcement of its outcome.

Scene three, 19:19–21.

The third scene also begins *kai eidon*/"then I saw." John sees the beast and the kings of the earth with their armies gathered to make war against the warrior messiah and his hosts. (Remember 16:14–16?) Again, only the outcome is given: "And the beast was captured, and with it the false prophet" (13:1–10, 11–18). These two were thrown alive into the lake of fire; the rest were slain by the warrior messiah. "And all the birds were gorged with their flesh" (v. 21b) (= the number of enemies defeated is very large). Scenes one, two, and three combine to describe the parousia of Christ and its victory over the forces of evil. One enemy of God, however, remains as yet unscathed: the dragon. What of him?

Scene four, 20:1–3.

The fourth scene also begins with *kai eidon*/"then I saw." In this scene John sees an angel coming down from heaven with the key to the bottomless pit (= the place of confinement of evil spirits awaiting judgment, 1 Enoch 88:1; Jubilees 5:6; Luke 8:31; Jude 6) and with a great chain: "And he seized the dragon, that ancient serpent, who is the Devil and Satan, and bound him for a thousand years, and threw him into the pit, and shut and sealed it over him, till the thousand years were ended" (v. 2). Ancient Judaism knew of a temporary binding of evil powers before the final judgment (Isa. 24:21–22; 1 Enoch 10:4–10; 18:12–16; 21:1–6; 54:5–6; Jubilees 5:10; T. Levi 18:12). This paragraph in Revelation assumes such a binding for the leader of the forces of evil and regards it as part of the aftermath of Christ's parousia. It is different from the casting down of the dragon after Christ's exaltation (12:7–9). Revelation 20:1–3, together with 20:4–6, has always been one of the most debated issues in Christian eschatology. Before it is discussed, however, it would be better to survey the next scene.

Scene five, 20:4–10.

Like the other scenes, scene five begins with *kai eidon/*"then I saw." It consists of two parts: vv. 4–6, which speak about the time of the thousand years when Satan is bound, and vv. 7–10, which refer to the period after Satan has been released.

During the period when Satan is bound (vv. 4–6), John's vision focuses on those who share in the millenial reign of Christ. Three questions are answered: Who are they? What do they do? How did they get here?

Those who participate in the thousand-year reign are those "who had been beheaded for their testimony to Jesus and for the word of God" (= Christian martyrs) *and* those who "did not worship the beast or its image and did not receive its mark upon their foreheads or their hands" (= non-martyrs who did not assimilate to Roman imperial power). There are two groups mentioned.[45] What they have in common is that they conquered; they did not worship the emperor. What distinguishes them is that some are martyrs, some are not.

These conquerors have two functions: they reign with Christ a thousand years (20:4b, 6b), and they serve as priests of God and Christ (v. 6). It is the reign that is associated with the thrones: "And I saw thrones, and seated on them were those to whom judgment was committed" (v. 4). It was early Christian belief that the saints would share in the judgment (1 Cor. 4:8; 6:2–3; Matt. 19:28; for a Jewish belief of a similar nature, cf. Testament of Abraham where each person is judged by Abel, by the twelve tribes of Israel, and by God; cf. also Wisd. Sol. 3:7–8; Sir. 4:11, 15; Jubilees 24:29; 1 QpHab 5:4–5). So here. It was also early Christian belief that the saints function as priests (1 Peter 2:9, "a royal priesthood . . . that you may declare the wonderful deeds of Him who called you out of darkness into His marvelous light"). The saints who share the millenial kingdom both share in the judgment of non-Christians and bear witness to Jesus.

The way to participate in the thousand-year reign of Christ is to share in the first resurrection. The rest of the dead (= non-Christian dead) "did not come to life until the thousand years were ended" (v. 5). It is implied here that the rest of the dead (= the non-Christians) will be raised after the thousand-year reign (as in fact they are in Rev. 20:12, although the term "second resurrection" is not used).

After the thousand-year period is ended, Satan is loosed from his prison and comes out to deceive the nations and to gather them for battle (20:7–8). In 19:11–21 the auditors have already heard of one battle, that associated with the parousia of Christ; now they hear of yet another war, that following the millenium. Satan gathers the nations that are at the four corners of the earth (= all the nations), that is, Gog and Magog (= the archetypal enemies of God in the last battle, as described by Ezekiel 38–39): "And they marched up over the broad earth and surrounded the camp of the saints and the beloved city" (20:9). The great eschatological war against Israel is a conventional feature of apocalyptic thinking (1 Enoch 56:5–8; 90:13–15; 4 Ezra 13:1–12; T. Joseph 19:8; Sib. Or. 3.662–701; 5.420–33; remember Rev. 16:12–16). The results are disastrous for all God's enemies: "fire came down from heaven and consumed them" (20:9b). The defeat of the evil forces is due to God's direct intervention. Defeat this time includes the devil: "and the devil who had deceived them was thrown into the lake of fire and sulphur where the beast and the false prophet were, and they will be tormented day and night for ever and ever" (v. 10).

There are two basic readings of scenes four and five (20:1–3, 4–10).[46] The first takes the millenium to refer to an actual reign of Christ and faithful Christians (those living and those raised) on earth for a thousand years, after the parousia (19:11–21) and before the last judgment (20:11–15). This has roots that go back at least to the early second century:[47] for example, the Ebionites (Jerome, *In Isaiah* 66.20); Cerinthus (so Eusebius, *Church History* 7.25; Epistle of Barnabas 15); Papias (so Eusebius, *Church History* 3.39.12); Justin Martyr, *Dialogue* 80–81; 65:17–25; Apocalypse of Peter; Ascension of Isaiah 4:14–17; Irenaeus, *Against Heresies* 5.35.2 (also Eusebius, *Church History.* 3.39.13); Tertullian, *Against Marcion* 3.25; Nepos, a bishop in Egypt in the time of Emperor Gallienus (Eusebius, *Church History* 7.24); Lactantius, *Divine Institutes* 7.26.

The other is hostile to the notion of a thousand-year reign on earth. It includes such ancient noteworthies as Origen (*De Principiis* 2.11.2; *Commentary on Matthew* 17:35); Eusebius (*Church History* 7.24–25); and Jerome (*On Isaiah* 11:15–16; 35:10; 60:1; *On Jeremiah* 31:28; *On Zechariah* 14:18). The reading that came to be accepted as an alternative to the millenarian interpretation is that of Augustine (*City of God* 20). Although espoused earlier by Victorinus of Pettau (*Commentary on the Apocalypse of John* 20:1–3 and 20:4–5), it was its advocacy by Augustine that gave the ecclesiastical interpretation its lasting impact on the Western church. In this reading, the thousand years equal all the years of the Christian era (from the incarnation/exaltation of Jesus to his parousia). The first resurrection symbolizes Christians' being raised with Christ (= conversion, cf. Eph. 2:5–6; Col. 2:12). These two ancient readings dominate discussion of Revelation 20 to this day.[48]

An intelligent evaluation of these two options is impossible without some prior discussion of both the historical development of Jewish eschatology and the theological function of the millenium in Revelation in particular and in the New Testament in general. We may begin with a sketch of some developments within Jewish eschatology.

Jewish eschatology. There were, in ancient Judaism, two very different eschatologies (= views of the end): the prophetic and the apocalyptic. In the prophetic eschatology, the golden future was viewed as taking place on this earth within time and space as we know them and involving those who were then alive when the golden age occurred (e.g., Psalms of Solomon 17, 18; Testaments of the Twelve Patriarchs [T. Reuben 6:10–12; T. Simeon 5:5; T. Levi 8:11–15]; Sib. Or. 3.701–61, 767–95). In apocalyptic eschatology, the golden future takes place in a new creation beyond time and space as we know them and involves only those who have been raised from the dead (e.g., Dan. 12; Testament of Moses 10). In some circles, however, there was an attempt to reconcile these two very different eschatologies. This was done in a synthesis that treated the prophetic vision of the future as a temporary messianic kingdom on earth prior to the eternal kingdom of God beyond the resurrection.[49]

The length of the temporary messianic kingdom varied among apocalyptic writings: e.g., 1 Enoch 91:11–14, 15–17 (the eighth and ninth weeks of world history); 4 Ezra 7:28–29, 31–44 (400 years); 2 Bar. 29:1–30:5; 40:3 (unspecified); 2 Enoch 33 (1000 years); Apocalypse of Elijah 5:36–39 (40 years). Among the rabbis, various durations of the temporary messianic kingdom are suggested: e.g., Akiba (40 years), Jose the Galilean (60 years), Eleazar b. Azariah (70 years), Dosa (600 years), Eliezer b. Jose the Galilean (1000 years), Abbahu (7000 years).[50] From this diversity, it is evident that the duration is a multiple of ten and so a symbolic number (a long time, a little longer time, a considerably longer time, a very long time, etc.).

These three eschatologies existed side by side within the Jewish community at the beginning of our era. Sometimes, within the same writing multiple views of the future can be found. For example, in 2 Baruch, an apocalyptic writing composed of seven visions (1:1–9:2; 10:1–20:6; 21:1–34:1; 35:1–47:1; 47:2–52:7; 53:1–77:17; 77:18–87:1), vision three (cf.

especially 26–30) and vision four (cf. especially 39–40) contain a temporary messianic kingdom prior to the eternal kingdom of God, whereas vision six (cf. especially 70–74) and vision five (cf. especially 48–51) do not. Vision six reflects prophetic eschatology, whereas vision five represents apocalyptic eschatology. Likewise, in 1 Enoch, an apocalyptic writing composed of five different works (1–36; 37–71; 72–82; 83–90; 91–108), the Apocalypse of Weeks (1 Enoch 93:1–10; 91:11–17) employs a temporary messianic kingdom, but the separate vision in 1 Enoch 90 does not and may very well reflect prophetic eschatology. It appears from such evidence that in some Jewish circles the three eschatologies were viewed as complementary, not exclusive.

The most natural way to read the material in Revelation is to see the seventh vision (19:11–22:5) as appropriating the eschatological synthesis known from certain Jewish apocalypses in which a temporary messianic kingdom (Rev. 20:1–6) precedes the eternal kingdom of God (Rev. 21:1–22:5). If so, this would also explain the two end time battles (19:11–21 and 20:7–10). Both prophetic and apocalyptic eschatologies assumed a final battle between God's enemies and God and His representatives. When the two eschatologies are synthesized in Revelation, a temporary messianic kingdom precedes the eternal kingdom of God. There is a final battle preceding each. In the first, the Messiah and the angels fight and win (19:14); in the second, God Himself intervenes directly (20:9b).

Such a synthesis would also explain the two resurrections. In 2 Baruch, which has a temporary messianic kingdom preceding the eternal kingdom of God, there are two stages of resurrection (50:2; 51:1–10). In the first, the earthly bodies of those raised are reconstituted for life in the messianic kingdom on earth, whereas for life in the eternal kingdom of God there is a transformation into immortality. The same scenario is also found in the Christian Apocalypse of Thomas. Against the background of the three-stage eschatological synthesis of ancient Judaism, Revelation 19:11–20:10 makes good sense. Revelation 20:1–6 is talking about a temporary messianic kingdom of a thousand years' duration on earth.

Theological function in Revelation. Having examined the historical development of eschatological thought in Judaism and its relevance for our understanding of Revelation's seventh vision, it now is necessary to consider the theological function of a temporary messianic kingdom both in the Apocalypse of John and in the New Testament generally. When reflecting on the theological function of a temporary messianic kingdom in Revelation, two levels must be considered: first, its function in vision seven (19:11–22:5), and second, its function in the Apocalypse as a whole.

The first level to be considered is the role of a temporary messianic kingdom in vision seven of Revelation. The purpose of Satan's being bound is stated explicitly: "that he should deceive the nations no more, till the thousand years were ended" (20:3). "When the thousand years are ended, Satan will be loosed . . . and will come out to deceive the nations" (20:7–8). The role of Satan that is focused upon here is that of the deception of the world (John 8:44). During the millenium he will be unable to deceive. It will be a deception-free period. During this time when Satan is unable to deceive the world, the saints are exalted/vindicated by God ("I saw thrones, and seated on them were those to whom judgment was committed," 20:4), Christ reigns (v. 4), and the saints, as priests, proclaim the wonderful deeds of God (v. 6). In other words, this is a time when the gospel is preached in a way that makes it perfectly clear that it is true. And there is no deceiver to say otherwise! Nevertheless, when the thousand years are ended and the deceiver is again loosed, the nations follow Satan's leadership, gather for battle, and march against the camp of the saints (v. 8). What is the point?

The thousand-year reign without the deceiver and with God's will for history made perfectly clear shows that God deals with humans so as to leave them without excuse.[51] Earlier visions in Revelation have shown that the tribulation/judgment within history, designed to elicit repentance from human beings, has failed in its purpose (Rev. 9:20–21; 16:9, 11, 21). Now, in vision seven, God goes to extreme lengths. He binds the deceiver and sets up a period of time in which His will is perfectly clear and obvious to all. The hope is that to do so will elicit the repentance of the nations. Nevertheless, it is all to no avail. When the deceiver is set free, he still finds the hearts of humans responsive to his seductions. The millenium proves, then, that humans cannot blame their sinfulness on their environment or circumstances. The radical evil of the human heart is exposed. We are without excuse. The thousand-year reign brings to completion the motif in the Apocalypse that although God acts in history to redeem humans, His activity is frustrated by the depth of evil in human hearts. To this point, the argument has been historical and descriptive only. From this point, it will include hermeneutical issues as well (= How does one move from a description of what the text says to a constructive theological position for today?).

The second level to be considered is the role of the temporary messianic kingdom in Revelation as a whole. The Apocalypse is composed of seven visions of the end times (4:1–8:1; 8:2–11:18; 11:19–13:18; 14:1–20; 15:1–16:21; 17:1–19:5; 19:6–22:5). These seven visions repeat again and again the same basic material (the shift of the ages): repetition with variation (= recapitulation). In only one of these seven visions, the last, is there any reference to a temporary messianic kingdom. In the first, the movement is from tribulation, through judgment, to primeval silence (6:1–8:1); in the second, there is tribulation followed by judgment (8:6–11:18); in the fourth, there is judgment within history followed by judgment at the end of history (14:6–20); in the fifth, there is wrath within history followed by wrath at the end of history (16:1–21). Just as in certain Jewish apocalypses already mentioned, Revelation allows different visions of the end to lie alongside one another. They are complementary, not mutually exclusive, pictures of end-time events.[52]

The diversity offered in the visions of the end is analogous to the diversity of the Old Testament's portrayals of creation (e.g., Gen. 1:1–2:3; 2:4–24; Ps. 74:12–17; Ps. 104). Neither the biblical depictions of our ultimate origins nor those of our ultimate destiny reflect any uniformity in details. Poetic portrayals vary, as they emphasize first one and then another theological aspect of the whole truth about our ultimate origins and our ultimate destiny. To force poetic visions to conform to our expectations of scientific description is to violate the genre of the material. One would not say that Genesis's view of creation is that of the seven days in Gen. 1:1–2:3, anymore than one might claim that of Gen. 2:4–24 as Genesis's view; so, given the varied pictures of the end in Revelation, one would not claim vision seven is *the* view of the Apocalypse of John. Genesis's view of creation is known only from the synthesis of Gen. 1:1–2:3 and 2:4–24, not from the isolated details of either the one part or the other. Likewise, Revelation's picture of our ultimate destiny is not known from the details of any one of its seven parts, but only from the totality of its seven visions when taken together.

What is the theological function of a temporary messianic kingdom in the New Testament as a whole? Nowhere else in the New Testament is a temporary messianic kingdom after the parousia and before the last judgment ever mentioned. The only place other than in Rev. 20:1–6 that a temporary messianic kingdom is mentioned in the New Testament is 1 Cor. 15:20–28. There, in the context of affirming the future character of resurrection of Christians over against opponents with an over-realized eschatology, Paul frames his argument in terms of an apocalyptic scheme of stages in salvation history.[53] Christ's resurrection belongs to one stage (v. 20); the Christians' resurrection belongs to another (vv. 22b–23). Between Christ's resurrection and parousia is his heavenly rule: "For he must reign until he has put all enemies under his feet. The last enemy to be destroyed is death" (vv. 25–26). In this context, there is a messianic reign, but it is from heaven and is during the period between Jesus' resurrection and his parousia. This is certainly not the temporary messianic kingdom of Revelation 20, where Christ reigns on earth after his parousia and before the last judgment. A temporary messianic kingdom on earth after Jesus' parousia and before the last judgment is found in only one place in the New Testament. To say that Rev. 20:1–6 is the point of view of the New Testament is no more possible than to say that Ecclesiastes (or some other part, like the imprecatory Psalms) states the point of view of the Old Testament. Parts may contribute to the whole, but the whole cannot be reduced to one of its parts.

It is best to allow Rev. 20:1–6 its integrity and not try to explain it away as Augustine did and myriads today try to do, while at the same time refusing to allow the Apocalypse's perspective as a whole to be reduced to one part of it. It is also imperative that we allow the New Testament its integrity and not try to force it to conform in its various eschatological perspectives to that of Rev. 20:1–6. In other words, do not interpret Paul in terms of Revelation 20, and do not interpret Revelation 20 in terms of 1 Corinthians 15. Let each maintain the integrity of its own perspective. Then, when speaking about the New Testament perspective, treat the two visions of the future as you treat the two stories of creation in Gen. 1:1–2:3 and 2:4–24. Just as one's reading of Genesis 1 and 2 is not for the purpose of constructing a calendar of the events associated with our ultimate origins, so one's reading of Revelation 20 and 1 Corinthians 15 does not have as its aim the construction of a calendar of the events connected with the ultimate end. What is sought is truth of another type.

Scene six, 20:11–15.

This scene is also introduced by *kai eidon*/"then I saw." It is a picture of the last judgment. Like Dan. 7:9–10, Rev. 20:11–15's last judgment scene combines throne-books-fire (1 Enoch 47:3 combines throne-books). The paragraph deals with four questions: Who judges? Who is judged? On what basis is judgment made? and What is its outcome?

Who judges? "Then I saw a great white throne and Him who sat upon it; from His presence earth and sky fled away, and no place was found for them" (v. 11). God Himself judges (Dan. 7:9; 1 Enoch 60:2; 62:2).

Who is judged? "And I saw the dead, great and small, standing before the throne" (v. 12a); "and the sea gave up the dead in it, Death and Hades gave up the dead in them" (v. 13). All the dead are raised to stand before the throne (John 5:28–29; 1 Enoch 1:7; 25:4; 41:9; 2 Enoch 65:6; 2 Bar. 83:2).

On what basis is judgment made? "And the books were opened. Also another book was opened, which is the book of life (13:8). And the dead were judged by what was written in the books, by what they had done. . . . all were judged by what they had done. . . . and if any one's name was not found written in the book of life . . ." (vv. 12, 13b, 15a). There are two sets of books mentioned here. The first are the heavenly books in which the deeds of humans are recorded for judgment. These books are a part of

Jewish and Christian thought worlds (*Jewish*. Dan. 7:10; 4 Ezra 6:20; 2 Bar. 24:1, "For behold, the days are coming, and the books will be opened in which are written the sins of all those who have sinned"; 1 Enoch 104:7, "all your sins are being written down every day"; 1 Enoch 9:20–39; 47:3; 2 Enoch 19:5, "angels who record all human souls and all their deeds, and their lives before the face of the Lord"; Apocalypse of Zephaniah 3:6–9; 7:1–8; *Christian*. Ascension of Isaiah 9:22–23 speaks about heavenly books in which the deeds of people are written down).

The second is the book of life in which the names of the redeemed are inscribed. This book is also part of Jewish and Christian imagery (*Jewish*. Ex. 32:32–33; Ps. 69:28; Dan. 12:1; Mal. 3:16; 1 Enoch 104:1; Apocalypse of Zephaniah 3:7; *Christian*. Luke 10:20; Phil. 4:3; Heb. 12:23).

Judgment is on the basis of what is written in these two sets of books. These two sets of books symbolize a paradox. The names in the book of life have been written from before the foundation of the world (= divine election, 13:8); but only those who endure are written in the books of records (= human responsibility). All judgment scenes regard human responsibility as crucial (= judged by what they had done, 20:12b), but the book of life says that the ones who endured do so only because of God's grace. This is a paradox that can be resolved only when one goes back to one's own experience with God and finds divine grace and human responsibility bound together in an indissoluble union.

What is the outcome of judgment? "If any one's name was not found written in the book of life, he was thrown into the lake of fire, . . . the second death" (v. 15; Fragment Targum of the Pentateuch, Deut. 33:6, "May Reuben live in this world; and may he not die a second death, by which [death] the wicked die in the world to come")[54] along with death and Hades (v. 14). By implication, those whose names are written in the book of life and who have proved faithful, as evidenced by what is written in the books of record, are destined for the New Age about which we will hear in 21:1–22:5.

The Christian belief in a last judgment at which God settles accounts according to His standards and in His own way is decisive for human behavior. Luke Johnson put it succinctly:

> What follows when we deny the confession that God judges the world? First, we must assume the entire responsibility for justice being done in the world. . . . And since we have no heaven or hell, we must do it now. Vengeance is not only legitimated, it is demanded.[55]

Scene seven, 21:1–22:5.

Scene seven also begins *kai eidon/*"then I saw." This large scene falls into two parts: 21:1–8 and 21:9–22:5. Each of these parts begins with references to the "holy city, Jerusalem, coming down out of heaven from God" (vv. 2a and 10) and to the bride (vv. 2b and 9). Each mentions the benefits derived from having a part in the New Age (21:4, 5–8; 21:23–22:5). Within scene seven of vision seven, as well as among the seven visions themselves, there is repetition with variation.

Part one of scene seven (21:1–8) functions as an overview of the New Age. It addresses what the New Age includes (vv. 1, 2, 3, 4), who is responsible for its appearing (vv. 5a, 6), and who shares in it and who does not (vv. 7–8). There is also within it an assurance of the reliability of its report (v. 5b).

What does the New Creation include? First, there are a new heavens and a new earth (= a new environment; Isa. 65:17; 1 Enoch 45:4–5; 4 Ezra 7:75; 2 Bar. 32:6; 2 Peter 3:10–13), in which the sea (= the principle of chaos, disorder) is no more (Testament of Moses 10:6, "the sea shall return into the abyss"; Sib. Or. 5.447, "in the last time the sea shall be dry"; T. Levi 4:1).

Second, "the holy city, the new Jerusalem" comes down from God, prepared as a bride adorned for her husband (v. 2). Both ancient Jews and early Christians held an expectation that with the shift of the ages a new Jerusalem would appear.

Jewish. Isaiah 54:11–12 has God say this: "I will set your stones in antimony, and lay your foundations with sapphires. I will make your pinnacles of agate, your gates of carbuncles, and all your walls of precious stones." Tobit 13:16–17 says that in the last days Jerusalem will be built with sapphires and emeralds, her walls with precious stones, her towers and battlements with gold; her streets will be paved with beryl and ruby. In 5Q15, an angel leads the author into the new Jerusalem and measures the city. The streets are paved with white stone, marble, and jasper. It has twelve gates. There is a new temple in it. T. Dan 5:12 says the "righteous shall rejoice in the new Jerusalem." Sibylline Oracles 5.420–33 mentions a new city with a new temple. In 1 Enoch 90:29 it says the new house/city will be greater than the first. It will descend to earth on the last day. In 4 Ezra 7:26 it says that at the end "the city which now is not seen shall appear"; 8:52 says that the age to come is prepared, the tree of life is planted, and a city is built for God's people; 10:25–28, 44–59 has Ezra view the heavenly Jerusalem in a vision; 13:36 says that Zion will come and be made manifest to all people. In 2 Baruch 4:3–5 it says that the new Jerusalem is preserved with God until the end. From these selected examples, one can conclude that ancient Jews expected a new Jerusalem at the end time as part of God's provision for His people. It will be greater than the first, made of precious stones and metals.

Christian. Galatians 4:26 mentions the Jerusalem that is above (cf. Phil. 3:20). Hebrews 11:10; 12:22 speak about the heavenly Jerusalem; 13:14 refers to the city that is to come. Five Ezra 2:42–48 talks about a great multitude and the Messiah being on Mount Zion in the end times. The Apocalypse of Paul 23–24 mentions that the city of Christ, which is very large, is made of precious materials and is Eden reclaimed.

Revelation. In the Apocalypse of John the expectation of a new Jerusalem is transformed from a place for God's people into an image of God's people themselves (as in the Qumran document, 4QpIsd, where the new Jerusalem is the community itself).[56] The language about the city's being made of precious stones and metals is retained, as is the reference to its coming down from heaven at the end. In Revelation, the new Jerusalem is also linked to Eden imagery (as in Judaism in T. Dan 5:12 where "in Eden" and "in the new Jerusalem" are in synonymous parallelism). The purity of the new Jerusalem (= God's people) is compared to that of a bride adorned for her husband.

Third, the New Creation consists of God's tabernacling with humans: "Behold, the dwelling (*skēnē*) of God is with men. He will dwell (*skēnōsei*) with them, and they shall be His people, and God Himself will be with them" (Rev. 21:3; Lev. 26:11–12; Ezek. 37:27). This presence of God in the midst of His people is in stark contrast to the fate of Babylon (= Rome) in Rev. 18:2: "It has become a dwelling place of demons, a haunt of every foul spirit".

Fourth, in the New Age when the former things have passed away, "death shall be no more, neither shall there be mourning nor crying (Isa. 25:8; 35:10; 65:16–19; 1 Enoch 10:22) nor pain any more" (Rev. 21:4). The last enemy to be destroyed (1 Cor. 15:26) is banished to the lake of fire (Rev. 20:14). The New Age is free from death and its accompanying pain and suffering.

Who is responsible for the New Creation's appearing? "And He who sat upon the throne (4:2–3; 20:11) said, 'Behold, I make all things new'" (21:5a; Isa. 43:18–19; 65:17); "It is done (16:17)! I am the Alpha and the Omega, the beginning and the end. To the thirsty I will give from the fountain of the water of life without payment" (Rev. 21:6; Isa. 55:1). It is God who makes all things new (Rev. 11:15–18; 19:1–2).

Who shares in the New Age and who does not? "Those who conquer (Rev. 2:7b, 11b, 17b, 26a; 3:5a, 12a, 21a) shall have this heritage, and I will be their God and they shall be my children" (Rev. 21:7a). In Revelation, "to conquer" means to resist assimilation to Roman imperial culture and to persevere in first-commandment faithfulness to God/Christ. To such does the New Creation belong. However, "as for the cowardly, the faithless, the polluted, as for murderers, fornicators, sorcerers, idolaters, and all liars, their lot shall be in the lake that burns with fire and sulphur, which is the second death" (Rev. 21:8). This list would apply above all to Christians who have apostatized, but in addition, to pagans who shared in the idolatry of and the persecution by Roman imperial power.

The first part of scene seven also contains within it a statement of its reliability. God Himself says: "Write this, for these words are trustworthy and true" (Rev. 21:5b; 19:9; 22:6; Gal. 1:20; Heb. 6:13–14; Jer. 22:5).

Part two of scene seven (21:9–22:5) begins with one of the seven angels of 16:1–21 coming to the prophet John and making an offer: "Come, I will show you the Bride, the wife of the Lamb" (21:9); "And in the Spirit he carried me away . . . and showed me the holy city Jerusalem coming down out of heaven from God" (v. 10). This indicates that the focus of the second part of vision seven is on the new Jerusalem/the bride of Christ (= the faithful people of God). Part two starts with an ABA' pattern (vv. 12–21).

Verses 12–14, part A, begin with a description of the high wall (= perfect protection, Isa. 26:1; Zech. 2:5) whose foundations have on them the names of the twelve apostles (= apostolic basis), and of the twelve gates of the city (= abundant access), each guarded by an angel (Gen. 3:24), with the names of the twelve tribes of Israel on them (Ezek. 48:30–34; 2 Enoch 65:10). The church's identity (= boundaries and access) is here linked to the history of Israel and to the apostolic tradition.

Verses 15–17, part B, move to the measuring of the city by the angel (remember 5Q15). Two characteristics of the city emerge. The first is that "the city lies foursquare, its length the same as its breadth . . . its length and breadth and height are equal." The city is a perfect cube. The second is that the city is "twelve thousand stadia" (= about fifteen hundred miles). It is huge. Its great size implies that there is room for all the conquerors. What of its being a perfect cube? Herodotus (*History* 1.178) says that Babylon, which was regarded as the ideal city of its time, was a square. The Greeks regarded the square as a symbol of perfection (Plato, *Protagoras* 344A; Aristotle, *Rhetoric* 3.11.2). The Jewish Holy of Holies, however, was not just a square; it was a perfect cube (1 Kings 6:20, "the inner sanctuary was twenty cubits long, twenty cubits wide, and twenty cubits high"). The new Jerusalem is like the Holy of Holies, the place of God's tabernacling presence.

Verses 18–21, part A', return to a focus on the wall and gates of the city. Throughout, these verses speak about the materials of which the walls with their foundations, and the gates with their streets, are composed (= the beauty of the city; remember Isa. 54:11–12; Tobit 13:16–17; 5Q15).

The remaining verses of this part of vision seven also reflect an ABA' pattern: A, 21:22–27, three things not in the city; B, 22:1–2, two things in the city; A', 22:3–5, two things not in the city.

Part A, in 21:22–27, refers to three things not to be found in the New Jerusalem: no temple, no sun or moon, no unclean thing.

Jewish expectations for the New Creation often included not only a new Jerusalem but also a new temple in the city (1 Enoch 90:28–29; Jubilees 1:27; Tobit 13:16–18; 14:5; 11QTemple 29.8–10; 4QFlorilegium 1.1–3; 5Q15; Sib. Or. 5.420–33; Targum on Isaiah 53:5; Midrash on the Psalms 90:17). In Rev. 21:22, however, John says: "I saw no temple in the city, for its temple is the Lord God the Almighty and the Lamb."

"And the city has no need of sun or moon to shine upon it, for the glory of God is its light, and its lamp is the Lamb" (21:23); "and there shall be no night there" (21:25). "Nothing unclean shall enter it, nor any one who practices abominations or falsehood, but only those who are written in the Lamb's book of life" (21:27; Isa. 52:1). Although the gates are never shut (21:25), inside the walls are only the conquerors who are clad in white garments (3:5). There are insiders and outsiders in the new Jerusalem. The city is not infinitely inclusive.[57]

Part B, in 22:1–2, describes two things that are in the city: the river of the water of life (= life giving) "bright as crystal, flowing from the throne of God and of the Lamb (= life comes from the sovereignty of God and the Lamb) through the middle of the street of the city" (22:1–2a; 21:6), and "on either side of the river, the tree of life (= life giving) with its twelve kinds of fruit, yielding its fruit each month; and the leaves of the tree were for the healing of the nations" (22:2b; 2:7; 1 Enoch 25:5; 4 Ezra 8:52; 2 Enoch 8:3–4; T. Levi 18:11). The tree of life and the water of life echo Genesis 2. The assumed perspective of these verses is that immortality is not natural but is a conferred status, a gift of God. The explicit point of these verses is to say that paradise has been regained. As in some circles of Jewish life (e.g., T. Dan 5:12), here the metaphors of new Jerusalem and paradise/Eden flow together. The people of God in vision seven are like a city, like a bride, and like Eden.

Part A', in 22:3–5, returns to the theme of things that are not in the city. In these verses two things are mentioned: (1) no accursed thing (= under a curse or ban of destruction; Deut. 7:25–26, here because of its idolatrous nature; Zech. 14:11) because the throne of God is in the city and His servants worship him, and (2) no night: "And night shall be no more . . . for the Lord God will be their light" (Zech. 14:6–7; Isa. 60:19–20; 2 Bar. 48:50). In the garden, perfect provision is made for God's people.

How long will this glorious state of affairs last? "They shall rule for ever and ever" (Rev. 22:5b). For the auditors of the Apocalypse, the promise is given: their oppression is transient, their reign will be eternal. As Rev. 21:7–8 reminds us, this grand picture is offered as an incentive for first-Commandment faithfulness in the present.

The seven visions are complete. All that remains is an epilogue (Rev. 22:6–21). To that we now turn.

4

EPILOGUE
(22:6–21)

Revelation begins with seven letters to seven churches in the province of Asia (2:1–3:22). It continues with seven visions of the end times (4:1–22:5). It ends with an epilogue (22:6–21). This closing section now receives our attention.

THE COMPONENTS OF THE EPILOGUE

The first question that arises for anyone who reads the epilogue is this: Who is speaking? About some of the sections there is no doubt:

v. 7a, b	= the risen Christ
v. 8	= the prophet John
v. 9	= the revealing angel
vv. 12–13	= the risen Christ
v. 16	= the risen Christ
v. 17a	= the Holy Spirit and the church
vv. 18–19	= the author
v. 20a	= the risen Christ
v. 20b	= the church
v. 21	= the author.

About some sections there is uncertainty.

Who is speaking in v. 6?—the angel of 21:9–22:5 or the risen Christ of 1:11, 19? Scholars differ, but it seems to me that the preferable choice is the risen Christ. In 22:6 the risen Christ picks up where he had left off in chap. 1. If so, then in vv. 6–7 Christ is speaking.

Who speaks in vv. 10–11? Is it the angel of 21:9–22:5 or Christ? Opinions vary. It seems to me most natural to assume the angel of v. 9 continues. If so, then in vv. 9–11 the angel is speaking.

104

Who speaks in vv. 14–15? Is it Christ or the angel? It seems natural to me to see these verses as a continuation of Christ's words in vv. 12–13. If so, then vv. 12–15 are spoken by the risen Christ.

Who is speaking in v. 17b, c? The Spirit and the Church speak in v. 17a; 17b, c are first an exhortation to the auditors to issue an invitation and then an invitation issued by the speaker. Both seem to me best understood as coming from the author. If so, then vv. 17b–19 are from the author.

These suggestions yield results that look like this:

vv. 6–7	= the risen Christ (three logia)
v. 8	= John
vv. 9–11	= the angel (two groups of two logia each)
vv. 12–16	= the risen Christ (six logia in three groups)
v. 17a	= the Spirit and the church
vv. 17b–19	= the author
v. 20a	= the risen Christ
v. 20b	= the church
v. 21	= the author.

On the basis of these conclusions, let us examine the individual parts of the epilogue.

The first component, 21:6–7.

The first component of the epilogue, 21:6–7, consists of three logia of the risen Christ. Verse 6 is concerned with the authenticity of the book. It offers a testimony of truthfulness ("These words are trustworthy and true"; cf. 19:9b; 21:5b) followed by the basis for its veracity ("The Lord, the God of the spirits of the prophets, has sent His angel to show His servants what must soon take place"; cf. 1:1). The book is truthful because it rests on a revelation from God.

Verse 7a is a promise: "Behold, I am coming soon" (1:1; 2:16; 3:11; 22:6, 12, 20). It functions as the basis for what follows in v. 7b.

Verse 7b is a beatitude: "Blessed are (= congratulations to) those who keep the words of the prophecy of this book" (1:3). It functions as an exhortation: "Keep the words of the prophecy" (because Jesus is coming soon).

The second component, 21:8.

The second component of the epilogue comes in v. 8. It is a word of John in two parts. The first ("I John am he who heard and saw these things") is the testimony of the recipient of the visions designed to support the veracity of what has been written (v. 8a). The second reflects the state of awe experienced by the recipient of the revelation ("I fell down to worship at the feet of the angel").

The third component, 21:9–11.

The third component, 21:9–11, consists of two groups of two logia each.

The first grouping (v. 9) is made up of a negative ("You must not do that") and its reason ("I am a fellow servant with you and your brethren the prophets"; cf. 19:10; Ascension of Isaiah 7:21; 8:4–5) and a positive ("Worship God"; 19:10). Worship belongs only to the Creator, not the created. Angels and prophets are but servants of God. Here John is regarded as one among a group of prophets. This raises the question of the shape of the ministry in the Apocalypse. Bishops, elders, deacons, deaconesses, and widows are not mentioned (contrast 1 Tim. 3:1–7; 5:17–20; Titus 1:5–9; 1 Tim. 3:8–10, 12–13; 1 Tim. 3:11; 1 Tim. 5:3–16). The apostles from the past are the foundation for the church (Rev. 21:14; cf. Eph. 2:20). The only functionaries mentioned for the church's present are prophets.

There are at least three types of ministry operative in early Christianity. The first is that of the charismatic leader whose authority is based on the work of the Spirit. Jesus certainly falls into this camp (cf. Matt. 7:28–29; Luke 4:16–21), as does Paul (Gal. 1:15–17; 1 Cor. 9:1–2). From the period at the end of the first or the beginning of the second century, the Didache 11–13 and 15:1–2 offer evidence of wandering prophets who sometimes settle in a given locale for a period of time. It is these figures who have the greatest status in the churches.

A second kind of ministry is that of the leader who operates with a delegated authority. From the period before Jesus' death, one can cite Mark 6:7–13 and Luke 10:16 as describing this. From the period after Easter, Acts 1:15–26, 14:23 and 20:17–35 offer examples. From the end of the first century, 2 Tim. 1:12, 1:13–14, 2:2, and 1 Clement 42:1–5 reflect delegated authority. One's authority for ministry is delegated either by Jesus or by some apostle.

A third type of ministry found in the early church is hereditary authority. Here transmission of authority is based on family ties. The depiction of James, the brother of Jesus, as the "bishop" of the Jerusalem church in Acts 15 is illustrative. Eusebius (*Church History*, 3.11 and 4.22.4) says that after James's martyrdom, Symeon, a cousin of Jesus, became bishop in Jerusalem. In 3.20.6 and 3.22.5–6, Eusebius says that still other relatives of Jesus presided over various other churches in Palestine until the time of Trajan. Apparently family ties determined ecclesiastical leadership. In Revelation the dominance of prophets, taken together with the absence of reference to other types of ministries, leads to the conclusion that the

Apocalypse reflects a charismatic type of ministry. The churches are led by prophets.

The second grouping of vv. 9–11 and vv. 10–11, also consists of a negative ("Do not seal up the words of the prophecy of this book") and its reason ("for the time is near"), and a positive ("Let the evildoer still do evil, and the filthy still be filthy, and the righteous still do right, and the holy still be holy"). The negative and its reason stand in contrast with Dan. 8:26 ("seal up the vision, for it pertains to many days hence"), Dan. 12:4 ("shut up the words, and seal the book, until the time of the end"), and Dan. 12:9 ("the words are shut up and sealed until the end of time"). In the one case, the vision is sealed (= not accessible to all) because the end is not near; in the other case, the vision is not to be sealed (= it is to be accessible to all) because the end is near. The delay in the coming of the end has been due to God's desire that the wicked repent (Rev. 9:20–21; 16:9, 11, 21; 20:1–10; Rom. 2:4–5; 2 Pet. 3:9). Now, however, the end is at hand, and people will just have to face it, whatever their present condition may be.

The fourth component, 21:12–16.

The fourth component in the epilogue, 21:12–16, consists of six logia of the risen Christ in three groups of two each. The three groups are arranged in an ABA' pattern. Parts A and A' both have two "I sayings"; B contains third-person statements.

Part A, vv. 12–13, begins with two "I sayings," the second giving the basis for the first: (1) "Behold, I am coming soon, bringing my recompense, to repay everybody for what they have done" (v. 12; vv. 7a, 20; cf. 16:15) and (2) "I am the Alpha (= the A) and the Omega (= the Z), the first and the last, the beginning and the end" (= a claim to deity, cf. 1:8; Isa. 41:4; 44:6; also Eusebius, *Preparation for the Gospel* 3.9, cites an ancient hymn to Zeus in which he is acclaimed: "Zeus first, Zeus last"). Christ will be judge because he is divine.

Part B, vv. 14–15, is composed of two third-person sayings that establish who are insiders and who are outsiders in the New Creation: (1) a beatitude defining insiders as those who are pure/non-assimilators ("Blessed are those who wash their robes [3:5; 19:8], that they may have the right to the tree of life [3:7] and that they may enter the city by the gates"; 21:7) and (2) a vice list defining outsiders as those who assimilate into Roman imperial culture ("Outside are the dogs and sorcerers and fornicators and murderers and idolaters, and every one who loves and practices falsehood"; cf. 21:8).

Part A', v. 16, consists of two "I sayings," the second giving the basis for the first: (1) "I Jesus have sent my angel to you with this testimony for the churches" (Rev. 22:6) and (2) "I am the root and offspring of David (Rev. 5:5; Isa. 11:1, 10), the bright morning star" (Rev. 2:28; 21:23b). As Messiah, Jesus can send his angel with a revelation for the churches.

The fifth component, 21:17a.

The fifth component is a simple invitation: "The Spirit and the Bride say, 'Come.'" The invitation is addressed to any and all auditors who need to be attached to Jesus and to share in the New Creation/new Jerusalem/paradise regained. The Holy Spirit (= here, the Spirit of prophecy) and the church issue the invitation.

The sixth component, 21:17b–19.

Component six in the epilogue derives from the author. It consists of an exhortation, an invitation, and a warning. Verse 17b is an *exhortation* addressed to the auditors: "Let those who hear say, 'Come.'" The auditors should join the Spirit of prophecy and the church in issuing an invitation to the spiritually needy. Verse 17c is an *invitation* issued by the author: "Let those who are thirsty come, and let those who desire take the water of life without price" (Isa. 55:1). Verses 18–19 are a *warning* against tampering with the words of the prophecy ("if anyone adds to them, God will add to him the plagues described in this book, and if anyone takes away from the words . . . , God will take away his share in the tree of life and in the holy city").

In antiquity there are found numerous prohibitions against tampering: Ezra 6:11–12 says a king's edict is not to be altered; 1 Enoch 104:10–11 predicts that sinners will alter Enoch's words; and 2 Enoch 48:6–8 says that the way people treat Enoch's words (that is, preserve or tamper with them) reveals whether they are just or unjust. Irenaeus (Eusebius, *Church History* 5.20.2) says at the end of his book *On the Ogdoad* that whoever copied it should transcribe it intact. Aristeas 310–311 says that the LXX translation was to be subject to no revision. A curse is laid on anyone who should alter it by addition, change, or deletion. Didache 4:13 instructs its readers not to add to or to take from the commandments of the Lord Jesus. It is in this context that Rev. 22:18–19 should be understood. Any communication is liable to corruption, be it a king's edict, an author's book, a prophet's message, Old Testament scripture, or Jesus' words. Given the normal proclivity, authors often inserted a command not to alter their communique. The presence of such a command, in itself, does not indicate that the author regarded the communique as scripture. The common proclivity to change was believed to be enhanced by the sinfulness of the last days that were characterized by corruption of prophecy (Ascension of Isaiah 3:21–31). It is within such a context that John wrote as he did.

The seventh component, 21:20a.

The seventh component repeats a saying of the risen Christ heard twice already in the epilogue (22:7a, 12): "Surely I am coming soon." The end is at hand.

The eighth component, 21:20b.

The eighth component is the church's answering prayer to Jesus' promise of a speedy parousia: "Amen (= so let it be). Come, Lord Jesus" (= perhaps the earliest Christian prayer we possess; cf. 1 Cor. 16:22b; Didache 10:6).

The ninth component, 21:21.

The ninth component in the epilogue is the author's benediction: "The grace of the Lord Jesus be with all the saints" (cf. 1 Cor. 16:23; Eph. 6:24). For an Apocalypse to end with a benediction is unusual. Its presence here is likely due to the fact that the apocalyptic visions are enclosed in a letter envelope (remember 1:4–8).

The epilogue to Revelation focuses two things for the auditors at the end of the visions: the Christ who stands behind the revelation is the one who is coming soon and the prophecy is crucial for the churches' behavior. This, then, is an appropriate place to summarize briefly Revelation's Christology and ethics.

Any overview of the Christology of the Apocalypse must pay attention both to the faces and the functions of Jesus.

The faces. There are two faces of Christ in Revelation. On the one hand, Jesus is clearly regarded as divine in the document. God and Jesus are often paralleled in such a way that the deity of Christ is a necessary inference. In 22:6, it is God who has sent His angel with the revelation; in 22:16, it is Jesus who has sent the angel. In 1:8, God is the Alpha and Omega; in 22:13 it is Jesus. In 5:13 and 22:3 one reads about the throne of God and the Lamb. In 11:15 one reads about the kingdom of God and Christ. It is clear that the author of Revelation treats Jesus as divine.

On the other hand, the Apocalypse implies continuity between the risen and coming Lord and the pre-Easter Jesus. In 5:5–6, 12, the Lamb who is about to open the seven seals is described as the one who has been slain. The use in Revelation of sayings for the risen Lord that echo sayings in the gospels of the pre-Easter Jesus establish the same continuity (Rev. 1:3, cf. Luke 11:28; 1:7, cf. Matt. 24:30; 3:2–3, cf. Matt. 24:42–44; 3:5, cf. Matt. 10:32; 3:20, cf. Luke 12:36–37; 3:21, cf. Luke 22:28–30; 13:10, cf. Matt. 26:52).[1] The pre-Easter Jesus and the risen Christ are the same person.

The functions. The functions of Christ in Revelation are best summarized in terms of past, present, and future tenses. When Jesus' past is noted there, Revelation focuses on his saving death (1:5, 18; 5:6, 9) and his victorious resurrection (1:5, 18; 5:5). In the present Jesus is understood as a revealer of God's plan for history (1:1; 22:16) and as the agent who sets in motion God's will upon the earth so that the New Creation will come (6:1–8:1). In depictions of the future, Revelation sees Jesus as the warrior Messiah at the parousia (19:11–16; 17:14), as the reigning ruler during the millenium (20:6; 12:5; 11:15), and as the bridegroom during the eternal kingdom of God (19:7, 9; 21:9–14).[2]

What does it means to keep the words of the prophecy of this book (22:7b), to do right and be holy still (22:11), and to wash one's robes (22:14)? This raises the whole issue of the ethics of Revelation.[3] Any such discussion must focus on two issues: what humans are asked to do and what God does to facilitate it.

What humans are asked to do. To those who are living unfaithfully (= assimilating to Roman imperial culture), the call is to repent (2:5, 21; 3:3, 19; 9:20–21; 18:4–5; 22:14 [cf. 7:14]; and 22:17). To those who are living faithfully (= refusing to assimilate), the encouragement is to endure faithfully (2:3, 7, 10, 11, 17, 26; 3:5, 12, 21; 13:10b; 14:4–5, 13; 16:15; 18:4–5; 22:7b).

What God does to facilitate it. To enable repentance, God does two things. First, He sends suffering (3:19) during history (cf. 9:20–21 in the context of 8:2–11:18; 16:8–9, 10–11, 21, in the context of 16:1–21). An analogy is present with the function of the plagues in Egypt at the exodus, which were designed in part at least, to cause Pharoah to repent (Ex. 7:12, 22; 8:15, 19, 32; 9:7, 12, 35; 10:20, 27; 11:10). The tribulation/judgment within history, likewise, has a redemptive intent. Second, He provides a deception-free environment during the temporary messianic kingdom in the hope that when deception is absent, humans will be converted (20:1–10).

To enable patient endurance, God protects His people from apostasy during the tribulation (7:1–8, the sealing; 11:1–2, the measuring; 12:13–16, the protection).

To enable both repentance and patient endurance, God/Christ/the Spirit/angels provide promises (2:7, 11b, 17b, 26–28; 3:5, 12, 21; 14:13; 17:1; 21:6–8) and visions (6:12–17; 7:9–17; 11:15–18; 14:1–5, 9–11; 15:2–4; 16:5–7; 19:1–5; 20:4–6; 21:9–22:5) of the ultimate outcome of history.

John is addressing a Christian community that is in danger of losing its identity by assimilating into a society that is set in opposition to God and Christ. Revelation's ethical values reflect the prophet of Patmos's resistance to that problem. His ethical foci, repent and endure, take their meaning from the problem and function in the interests of first-commandment faithfulness. John's ethics reflect the paradox: repentance and endurance are the result both of what we do and what God enables.

THE RELEVANCE
OF REVELATION FOR TODAY

In this chapter of the book, it is necessary not only to give attention to the epilogue of the Apocalypse of John (22:6–21) but also to offer an epilogue of our own having to do with the relevance of Revelation for Christians today. In the opening chapter of this volume, it was noted that the Apocalypse is neglected by mainstream Christians today for three main reasons: the inaccessibility of its meaning; the absence of pastoral relevance; and its demonstrated susceptibility to abuse. The reading offered of Revelation to this point has attempted to show that, when read in the context of apocalyptic literature generally, Revelation's meaning is reasonably accessible. In this section, it is necessary to demonstrate the Apocalypse's pastoral relevance. Any such discussion must focus on two levels: the potential relevance of Revelation when taken alone and the volume's potential relevance when taken as a part of the entire Christian canon of scripture.

When taken alone, Revelation functions as an antidote to Christian assimilation into a culture with an alien ethos. Consider the historical *situation.* When the Apocalypse was written, some Christian leaders were eagerly advocating assimilation to statist society (= society with the ethos of state omnicompetence, in which the state is a quasi-religious agency, making decisions in arguably religious areas and producing its own normative conceptions of life-in-society). Other Christians were assimilating unthinkingly because of spiritual anemia. Like the proverbial frog in the kettle, they were unaware of their increasing peril.

Given this situation, consider the *prophetic response.* The response of the prisoner of Patmos must be looked at in terms of both his message and his medium. First, John's message is that assimilation is not a possible avenue of action for Christians, because the ethos of statist society and the ethos of Christian community are, at base, incompatible. Statist society, taken to its logical outcome, represents an alternate religion. Those who fail to worship within statist society's religious framework will experience the full force of that society's sanctions against them.

In addition, John's medium is apocalyptic. First, he says by means of his apocalyptic visions, that there is a great persecution coming, the tribulation that Jews and Christians have heard about. It will require single-minded devotion of Christians, if they are not to apostatize. God will offer His people spiritual protection during the suffering that will enable them to endure. Second, he says by means of his visions, there is judgment coming on statist society in the last days both within history, in an attempt to elicit repentance, and at the very last day, as a punishment for idolatry and persecution. Anyone who sells out to statist society will share in the same fate. Third, he says through his visions, there is a glorious future in store for God's people who have resisted assimilation to statist society.

The Apocalypse of John has pastoral relevance in any context where Christian assimilation into a culture with a non-Christian ethos is an issue. It speaks harshly to those so-called Christian prophets who eagerly advocate assimilation to an alien ethos as something compatible with Christian faith. It also speaks a word of warning to the unthinking mass of Christians who simply want to share in the economic fruits of Babylon's wealth and luxury and are quite willing to assimilate in order to reap the temporal benefits. Revelation addresses not so much those alienated from the larger society because they belong to the "have-nots" as it does those with upward social mobility who want to be totally immersed in the larger society and are consciously or unconsciously willing to lose their souls in order to do so.[4]

Early Christians reflect a variety of types of relations to non-Christian culture. In some circles there is evidence of Christians striving to gain social acceptance without sacrificing their distinctive convictions (e.g., 1 Peter; Epistle to Diognetus). Other circles attempt to live in quiet detachment from the world, concerned only with the unity and inner purity of the Christian community itself (e.g., the Johannine epistles; cf. Eusebius, *Church History* 3.19–20, for the attitude reflected by relatives of Jesus in the time of Domitian). In still other circles, assimilation into non-Christian culture is resisted even at the risk of economic loss and/or martyrdom (e.g., Revelation).

These varying types of relations to culture reflect the differing circumstances of different times and places. When the church finds itself in a situation where statism characterizes the cultural context, where the mass of Christians desire full participation in the economic benefits of the culture even if it means the loss of their religious convictions, and where many of their leaders actively function as prophets for the values of the statist enterprise, then Revelation has a clear word for God's people. There is then pastoral relevance in the message of the Apocalypse of John when taken alone.

When read as a part of the larger canon of Christian scripture,[5] *Revelation functions to give assurance about the ultimate outcome of all things.* Christian scripture includes the two testaments: the Old Testament and the New Testament. There is a theological plot that controls the diversity of these two testaments. The plot runs thus: Creation, Fall, Covenant, Christ, Church, Consummation. Every part of the canon must be read within this overall plot or design.

How does the Apocalypse fit into this design of scripture? Just as the plot begins with a section on our ultimate origins (= Creation, Genesis 1–11), so it ends with a section on our ultimate destiny (= the New Creation, Revelation). Of course, references to Creation are not limited to the early chapters of Genesis and mention of the New Creation is not restricted to Revelation. Nevertheless, statements about our ultimate origins are focused in the early chapters of Genesis at the beginning of the canon to set the plot in motion, just as references to our ultimate destiny are focused at the end of the canon in the Apocalypse of John to give the plot its designed outcome. Taken as part of the Christian canon as a whole, Revelation functions as an affirmation of God's final word regarding His creation. What is the beginning of all things? The canon says: "In the beginning, God . . ." (Gen. 1:1a). What is the end of all things? The canon says: In the end, ". . . the throne of God and of the Lamb . . ." (Rev. 22:3a).

There is pastoral relevance in Revelation's message taken as part of the canon as a whole whenever Christians find themselves falling for the lie that "what is" is all there is, that the beast is all-powerful, and that no one can fight against him.[6] In such a context, the prophet of Patmos speaks a word of warning and of assurance. On the one hand, it is a word of warning to those who, because of loss of any sense of a destiny beyond this present evil age, accommodate themselves to the ethos of a non-Christian culture. It is a warning that those who worship the beast will share his fate. The fate of beast and worshipers alike will be dire because in the end God has the final word.[7] On the other hand, it is a word of assurance to those who, because of God's sustaining grace (= His sealing of the saints, measuring of the temple), resist accommodation to a society behind which stands the great red dragon. It is assurance that those who die in the Lord are blessed. They are blessed because in the end God has the final word.

But, many readers will protest at this point, where are the references to the pre-, post-, or mid-tribulation rapture of the church? Where are the references to Middle East events that will involve the nation Israel and a possible oil war with tanks and atomic bombs? If the reader has sensed by this point that these items are missing from the reading of Revelation offered here, he/she has read this book carefully. Such items are not here.

They are not here because, if the Apocalypse of John is studied in the context of the ancient Jewish and early Christian apocalypses that are extant and available even to English-speaking readers, these items simply are not in Revelation. Only if one brings such a system to Revelation can the document be forced to yield alleged information on such matters. In that case, however, one is reading these matters *into* Revelation and not *out of* it.[8] Read in the context of the other ancient apocalypses, Revelation is an anti-assimilationist tract designed to inculcate first-commandment faithfulness among its auditors. Heard in this way, the Apocalypse of John is preserved from the abuse it so often suffers at the hands of its interpreters.

NOTES

1. GETTING STARTED

1. Adela Yarbro Collins, "Revelation, Book of," *Anchor Bible Dictionary*, ed. David Noel Freedman (New York: Doubleday, 1992), 5.702–3.

2. David L. Barr, "The Apocalypse of John as Oral Enactment," *Interpretation* 40 (1986): 243–56.

3. John J. Collins, "Introduction: Towards the Morphology of a Genre," *Semeia* 14 (1979): 9.

4. A. Y. Collins, "Introduction," *Semeia* 36 (1986): 7.

5. A. Y. Collins, "Early Christian Apocalypses," *Semeia* 14 (1979): 67.

6. For a comprehensive survey, see John J. Collins, "The Jewish Apocalypses," *Semeia* 14 (1979): 21–60.

7. A. Y. Collins, in "The Early Christian Apocalypses," *Semeia* 14 (1979): 61–122, offers a comprehensive survey.

8. A helpful reader that includes samples of both Jewish and Christian apocalypses, with introductions to assist one's understanding, is Mitchell G. Reddish, ed., *Apocalyptic Literature: A Reader* (Nashville: Abingdon, 1990). The standard exhaustive translation of Jewish apocalypses is James H. Charlesworth, ed., *The Old Testament Pseudepigrapha*, 2 vols. (Garden City, N.Y.: Doubleday, 1983). On Christian apocalypses, see Wilhelm Schneemelcher, ed., *New Testament Apocrypha*, vol. 2 (Philadelphia: Westminster Press, 1964). Gnostic apocalypses may be found in James M. Robinson, ed., *The Nag Hammadi Library in English* (San Francisco: Harper & Row, 1977).

9. *Anchor Bible Dictionary* 1.279–92.

10. L. L. Grabbe, "The Social Setting of Early Jewish Apocalypticism," *Journal for the Study of the Pseudepigrapha* 4 (1989): 27–47; Bengt Holmberg, *Sociology and the New Testament: An Appraisal* (Minneapolis: Fortress, 1990), 137–39 (appealing to Paul Hanson).

11. John J. Collins, *The Apocalyptic Imagination* (New York: Crossroad, 1984): 214.

12. Ray Summers, in *Worthy Is the Lamb: An Interpretation of Revelation* (Nashville: Broadman Press, 1951), 21–25, offers a helpful summary. The fullest treatment I know is that of A. Y. Collins, "Numerical Symbolism in Jewish and Early

Christian Apocalyptic Literature," in *Aufstieg und Niedergang der römischen Welt*, eds. H. Temporini and W. Haase, II.21.2, 1221–87.

13. On 2 Esdras 3–14 = 4 Ezra, cf. *Mercer Dictionary of the Bible*, ed. Watson Mills (Macon, Ga.: Mercer University Press, 1990), 286–87. On 2 Baruch, see F. J. Murphy, *The Structure and Meaning of Second Baruch* (Atlanta: Scholars Press, 1985), 12–13.

14. James L. Blevins, *Revelation as Drama* (Nashville: Broadman, 1984), understands the Apocalypse of John as an ancient drama. He therefore regards the visions of heavenly reality (e.g., Revelation 4–5; 8:5–6; 11:19; 15:5–8; 17:1–3) as stage settings.

15. Quoted by Bernard J. LeFrois, *The Woman Clothed with the Sun: Apocalypse 12* (Rome: Orbis Catholicus, 1954), 190. His debt is, of course, to Johannes Pedersen, *Israel: Its Life and Culture I–II* (London: Oxford University Press, 1926), 115, 123.

16. Bennison Gray, "Repetition in Oral Literature," *American Folklore* 84 (1971): 289–303, shows that oral literature is concerned with the ease with which it can be remembered. This accounts for its repetitiveness.

17. During the eighteenth and nineteenth centuries, most European scholars tended to date Revelation at the end of Nero's reign or during the reign of Galba (June 68–January 69). This dating is advocated today by J. Christian Wilson, "Some Reservations about the Domitianic Dating of Revelation," *New Testament Studies*, 39 (1993): 587–605.

18. Adela Yarbro Collins, "Dating the Apocalypse of John," *Biblical Research* 26 (1981): 33–45; *Crisis and Catharsis: The Power of the Apocalypse* (Philadelphia: Westminster Press, 1984), 70, 84–110.

19. R. H. Charles, *A Critical and Exegetical Commentary on the Revelation of St. John* (Edinburgh: T. & T. Clark, 1920); H. B. Swete, *The Apocalypse of John* (London: Macmillan, 1917); I. T. Beckwith, *The Apocalypse of St. John: Studies in Introduction with a Critical and Exegetical Commentary* (New York: Macmillan, 1919).

20. Leonard Thompson, "A Sociological Analysis of Tribulation in the Apocalypse of John," *Semeia* 36 (1986): 147–74; and *The Book of Revelation: Apocalypse and Empire* (New York: Oxford University Press, 1990). Hippolytus, *On the Twelve Apostles*, 5, does say that Philip, who preached in Phrygia, was crucified in Hierapolis with his head downward in the time of Domitian and was buried there. This need not mean more than that the populace took the initiative to charge him, that the governor then had to deal with the issue, and that when Philip refused to worship the emperor, he was crucified. Compare Pliny's Letter to Trajan for such a situation.

21. Martin Kiddle, *The Revelation to John* (New York: Harper, n.d.), xli, recognizes that John is anticipating the storm and is seeking to prepare his brethren before it breaks.

22. A. Y. Collins, "Coping with Hostility," *The Bible Today* 19 (1981): 367–72, and *Crisis and Catharsis: The Power of the Apocalypse* (Philadelphia: Westminster Press, 1984), chaps. 3 and 5.

23. Gerhard A. Krodel, *Augsburg Commentary on the New Testament: Revelation* (Minneapolis: Augsburg, 1989), 41, 355; Leonard Thompson, "A Sociological Analysis of Tribulation in the Apocalypse of John," *Semeia* 36 (1986): 162–66.

24. Carolyn Osiek, "The Genre and Function of the Shepherd of Hermas," *Semeia* 36 (1986): 118.

25. Gerhard A. Krodel, *Revelation*, 1989, 355.

26. Jan Lambrecht, in "A Structuration of Revelation 4:1–22:5," in *L'Apocalypse johannique et l'Apocalyptique dans le Nouveau Testament* (Leuven: University Press, 1980), 77–104, notes correctly that there are almost as many outlines of the book as there are interpreters. The outline I propose is not exactly like that of anyone else's. It contains nothing, however, that has not been suggested by one or more other scholars. It is with outlines as it is with pudding; the test is in the eating. Does it make reading easier or more difficult?

27. Revelation's resistance to Rome continues a long history of subject peoples' resistance to Hellenism. Compare Samuel K. Eddy, *The King Is Dead: Studies in Near Eastern Resistance to Hellenism 334–31 B.C.* (Lincoln: University of Nebraska Press, 1961).

2. THE SEVEN LETTERS TO THE SEVEN CHURCHES (1:1–8; 1:9–3:22)

1. Otto F. A. Meinardus, "The Christian Remains of the Seven Churches of the Apocalypse," *Biblical Archaeology* 37 (1974): 69–82.

2. On the place of the letters within the book, see Colin J. Hemer, *The Letters to the Seven Churches of Asia in Their Local Setting* (Sheffield, Eng.: JSOT Press, 1986); W. M. Ramsay, *The Letters to the Seven Churches of Asia and Their Place in the Plan of the Apocalypse* (reprint; Leiden: Brill, 1963); William Barclay, *Letters to the Seven Churches* (Nashville: Abingdon, 1957).

On the letters and their parallels, see D. E. Aune, "The Form and Function of the Proclamations to the Seven Churches (Revelation 2–3)," *New Testament Studies* 36 (1990): 182–204. It offers additional, non-Jewish parallels. His suggestion that the seven letters are more closely related to imperial edicts is debatable.

3. Elisabeth Schüssler Fiorenza, "Revelation, Book of," *Interpreter's Dictionary of the Bible, Supplement*, ed. Keith Crim (Nashville: Abingdon, 1976), 745.

4. A. Le Grys, in "Conflict and Vengeance in the Book of Revelation," *Expository Times* 104 (1992): 76–80, sees the Apocalypse as a response to false prophecy's claim that accommodation to the surrounding pagan culture supported by the state is theologically permissible.

5. Carolyn Osiek, "The Genre and Function of the Shepherd of Hermas," *Semeia* 36 (1986): 118.

6. Elisabeth Schüssler Fiorenza, in "Revelation," in *The New Testament and Its Modern Interpreters*, eds. Eldon Jay Epp and George W. MacRae (Atlanta: Scholars Press, 1989), 419, says, "The author appears to formulate this theology in opposition to an enthusiastic prophetic theology that seems to have advocated accommodation to the Roman civil religion. . . ."

3. THE SEVEN VISIONS OF THE END TIMES (4:1–22:5)

1. My practice is similar to that of Marie Isaacs, *Sacred Space: An Approach to the Theology of the Epistle to the Hebrews* (Sheffield, Eng.: JSOT Press, 1992), 67, n. 1: "The capitalization of personal pronouns for God adopted throughout this work is intended to signal that God is above gender—*not* that the deity is male." For my reservations about gender-inclusive language for God, see my essay "The

Church and Inclusive Language for God?" in *Perspectives on Contemporary New Testament Questions*, ed. Edgar V. McKnight (Lewiston, N.Y.: Edwin Mellen Press, 1992), 91–113.

2. Philip Edgcumbe Hughes, *The Book of Revelation: A Commentary* (Grand Rapids: Eerdmans, 1990), 78.

3. R. J. Bauckham, "The Worship of Jesus in Apocalyptic Christianity," *New Testament Studies* 27 (1980–81): 322–41. Christian worship for John and certain other early Christians did not extend to angels (Rev. 19:10; 22:8–9; Ascension of Isaiah 7:21–22; 8:5). The warning of Col. 2:18 and Justin Martyr's explicit statement (*1 Apology* 6:2 — God and the Son . . . and the army of other good angels who follow him and are made like him, and the prophetic Spirit, we worship and adore") indicate that some Christians did in fact worship angels.

4. Dale C. Allison, Jr., *The End of the Ages Has Come* (Philadelphia: Fortress Press, 1985), in chap. 2, "The Great Tribulation in Jewish Literature," offers a helpful survey. Compare also Robert H. Gundry, *The Church and the Tribulation* (Grand Rapids: Zondervan, 1973), and George E. Ladd, *The Last Things* (Grand Rapids: Eerdmans, 1978), 58–72.

5. J. P. Heil, "The Fifth Seal (Rev. 6:9–11) as a Key to the Book of Revelation," *Biblica* 74 (1993): 220–43.

6. So Kevin Lloyd (student paper for author's class, Religion 319, spring 1993).

7. M. Eugene Boring, *Revelation: Interpretation, A Bible Commentary for Teaching and Preaching* (Louisville: Westminster/John Knox, 1989), 128.

8. C. R. Smith, "The Portrayal of the Church as the New Israel in the Names and Order of the Tribes in Revelation 7:5–8," *Journal for the Study of the New Testament* 39 (1990): 111–18; R. Bauckham, "The List of the Tribes in Revelation 7 Again," *Journal for the Study of the New Testament* 42 (1991): 99–115.

9. Robert H. Mounce, *The Book of Revelation* (Grand Rapids: Eerdmans, 1977), 167–68; G. R. Beasley-Murray, *The Book of Revelation* (London: Oliphants, 1974), 140.

10. So Catie Luttrell (student paper for author's class, Religion 319, spring 1993).

11. The critique of the practice of Christian prayer as indifference to the plight of the world is addressed by William Johnston, *Being in Love: The Practice of Christian Prayer* (London: Fount Paperbacks, 1988), chap. 20, "Social Consciousness," 161–66.

12. Charles H. Talbert, *Learning through Suffering: The Educational Value of Suffering in the New Testament and in Its Milieu* (Collegeville, Minn.: Liturgical Press, 1991).

13. C. H. Giblin, "Revelation 11:1–13: Its Form, Function and Contextual Integration," *New Testament Studies* 30 (1984): 433–59.

14. André Feuillet, "The Messiah and His Mother according to Apocalypse 12," *Johannine Studies* (Staten Island, N.Y.: Alba House, 1965), 257–92; G. B. Caird, *Revelation* (London: Black, 1966), 148.

15. Dominique Cuss, *Imperial Cult and Honorary Terms in the New Testament* (Fribourg: University Press, 1974), 102.

16. Steven Friesen, "Ephesus: Key to a Vision in Revelation," *Biblical Archaeology Review*, (May–June 1993): 31–32.

17. Ibid., 36.

18. Richard Oster, "Christianity and Emperor Veneration in Ephesus: Iconography in Conflict," *Restoration Quarterly,* 25 (1982): 143–49.

19. Steven J. Scherrer, "Signs and Wonders in the Imperial Cult: A New Look at a Roman Religious Institution in the Light of Revelation 13:13–15," *Journal of Biblical Literature,* 103 (1984): 599–610. The following discussion is indebted to Scherrer.

20. Adolf Deissmann, *Light from the Ancient East,* rev. ed. (New York: Harper, 1922), 277–78.

21. I = 10; H = 8; S = 200; O = 70; Y = 400; S = 200.

22. David Brady, *The Contribution of British Writers between 1560 and 1830 to the Interpretation of Revelation 13:16–18 (The Number of the Beast): A Study in the History of Exegesis* (Tübingen: Mohr [Siebeck], 1983).

23. Oscar Cullmann, *The State in the New Testament* (New York: Charles Scribner's Sons, 1956), 86.

24. Henry J. Cadbury, *The Book of Acts in History* (London: Adam and Charles Black, 1955), 42–43.

25. John A. Bollier, "Judgment in the Apocalypse," *Interpretation* 7 (1953): 14–25; W. Klassen, "Vengeance in the Apocalypse of John," *Catholic Biblical Quarterly* 28 (1966): 300–11.

26. Charles H. Talbert, *Reading Luke* (New York: Crossroad, 1982), 87.

27. If one believes the entire book of Revelation is shaped by the motif of the holy war (as does C. H. Giblin, *The Book of Revelation* [Collegeville, Minn.: Liturgical Press, 1991]), then the other option might seem preferable.

28. Charles H. Talbert, *Reading John* (New York: Crossroad, 1992), 262.

29. D. S. Russell, *The Method and Message of Jewish Apocalyptic* (Philadelphia: Westminster Press, 1964), chap. 9, "Angels and Demons," 235–62.

30. M. Eugene Boring, in *Revelation: Interpretation* (Louisville: Westminster/John Knox, 1989, 226–31), claims some texts in Revelation "portray or imply universal salvation." The passages, when examined, have no such import. The attempt to read universal salvation into Revelation must be termed a failure. Whatever one's constructive theological posture based on the entirety of the canon, Revelation's posture is summed up in the phrase "for ever and ever," for righteous and wicked alike.

31. Sometimes Rev. 21:4 (death will be no more) and 21:14 (death is thrown into the lake of fire) are taken to imply annihilation. Death, however, is not a person. It is a personified result of sin. So its demise is not logically analogous to that of persons.

32. Ray Summers, *Worthy Is the Lamb: An Interpretation of Revelation* (Nashville: Broadman, 1951), 189.

33. Louis A. Vos, *The Synoptic Traditions in the Apocalypse* (Kampen: Kok, 1965).

34. Wilhelm Bousset, *The Antichrist Legend* (New York: AMS Press, 1982—reprint of 1896 ed.); Ernest Renan, *Antichrist* (Boston: Roberts Brothers, 1897); Gregory C. Jenks, *The Origins and Early Development of the Antichrist Myth* (Berlin: Walter de Gruyter, 1991).

35. Martin Kiddle, *The Revelation of St. John* (New York: Harper & Brothers, 1940), 350.

36. Cited by Richard Bauckham, *The Bible in Politics: How to Read the Bible Polit-*

ically (Louisville: Westminster/John Knox Press, 1990), 89, as the wording of a "grateful inscription at Halicarnassus, which celebrates the Emperor Augustus as 'saviour of the whole human race.'"

37. P. Aelius Aristides, *The Complete Works*, trans. C. A. Behr (Leiden: Brill, 1981), 2.75.

38. A. A. Trites, *"Martus* and Martyrdom in the Apocalypse: A Semantic Study," *Novum Testamentum* 15 (1973): 72–80; B. Dehandschutter, "The Meaning of Witness in the Apocalypse," in *L'Apocalypse johannique et l'Apocalyptique dans le Nouveau Testament*, ed. J. Lambrecht (Leuven: University Press, 1980), 283–88; M. G. Reddish, "Martyr Christology in the Apocalypse," *Journal for the Study of the New Testament* 33 (1988): 85–95.

39. Jenny Wallace, (student paper for author's class, Religion 319, spring 1993).

40. Gerhard Krodel, *Augsburg Commentary of the New Testament: Revelation* (Minneapolis: Augsburg, 1989), 126.

41. Contra Tina Pippin's *Death and Desire: The Rhetoric of Gender in the Apocalypse of John* (Louisville: Westminster/John Knox Press, 1992).

42. J. Fekkes, "'His Bride Has Prepared Herself': Revelation 19–21 and Isaian Nuptial Imagery," *Journal of Biblical Literature*, 109 (1990): 269–87.

43. G.W.H. Lampe, in "The Testimony of Jesus is the Spirit of Prophecy (Rev. 19:10)," *The New Testament Age*, ed. William Weinrich (Macon, Ga.: Mercer University Press, 1984), 1.245–58, says the angel is talking about the choice of confessing Christ in the face of persecution or of apostatizing.

44. Michael L. Klein, *The Fragment-Targums of the Pentateuch* (Rome: Biblical Institute Press, 1980), 2.119.

45. Philip Edgcumbe Hughes, *The Book of Revelation: A Commentary* (Grand Rapids: Eerdmans, 1990), 212; George R. Beasley-Murray, *The Book of Revelation* (London: Oliphants, 1974), 295.

46. Brian E. Daley, *The Hope of the Early Church* (Cambridge: Cambridge University Press, 1991).

47. Hans Bietenhard, "The Millenial Hope in the Early Church," *Scottish Journal of Theology* 6 (1953): 12–30.

48. A third option is that offered by Eugenio Corsini, *The Apocalypse: The Perennial Revelation of Jesus Christ* (Wilmington, Del.: Michael Glazier, 1983). Corsini says Revelation is about the first, not the second, coming of Christ. Hence, the chaining of Satan and the one thousand years are events that precede the coming of Christ in Bethlehem. The thousand years refer to the old covenant and the salvation attained through it. Chapters 21–22, the New Jerusalem, refer to the church militant within history between Christ's resurrection and parousia. Thus understood, Revelation does not introduce millenarianism but represents a reaction against it. This view has found little support within the scholarly community.

49. J. W. Bailey, "The Temporary Messianic Reign in the Literature of Early Judaism," *Journal of Biblical Literature* 53 (1934): 170–87.

50. George Beasley-Murray, *The Book of Revelation* (London: Oliphants, 1974), 288–89, lists these and other rabbis and their views about the time of the temporary messianic kingdom.

51. George Eldon Ladd, *A Commentary on the Revelation to John* (Grand Rapids: Eerdmans, 1972), 269.

52. Michael E. Stone, in "Coherence and Inconsistency in the Apocalypses: The Case of 'the End' in 4 Ezra," *Journal of Biblical Literature* 102 (1983): 229–43, wrestles with the issue in the context of Jewish apocalypses.

53. Charles H. Talbert, *Reading Corinthians* (New York: Crossroad, 1987), 98–99.

54. Michael L. Klein, *The Fragment Targums of the Pentateuch* (Rome: Biblical Institute Press, 1980), 2.188.

55. Luke T. Johnson, *Faith's Freedom: A Classic Spirituality for Contemporary Christians* (Philadelphia: Fortress, 1990), 23.

56. R. H. Gundry, "The New Jerusalem: People as Place, Not Place for People," *Novum Testamentum* 29 (1987): 254–64.

57. Richard B. Hays, in "An Emergency Directive," *Christian Century*, April 22, 1992, 425, says: "Infinite inclusivity trivializes the witness of the saints who have suffered for their refusal to worship the beast."

4. EPILOGUE
(22:6–21)

1. Louis A. Vos, *The Synoptic Traditions in the Apocalypse* (Kampen: Kok, 1965).

2. Donald E. Cook, "Christology in the Apocalypse," *The Outlook* 16 (1967): 3–9; Hans-Ruedi Weber, *The Way of the Lamb: Christ in the Apocalypse* (Geneva: WCC Publications, 1988).

3. Sean Smith, *Religion* 319 (spring 1993); Allen Verhey, *The Great Reversal: Ethics and the New Testament* (Grand Rapids: Eerdmans, 1984), 147–52; C. Freeman Sleeper, *The Bible and the Moral Life* (Louisville: Westminster/John Knox Press, 1992), 66–82.

4. This makes John's resistance a bit different from that chronicled by Samuel K. Eddy, *The King Is Dead: Studies in the Near Eastern Resistance to Hellenism 334–31 B.C.* (Lincoln: University of Nebraska Press, 1961). Of Eddy's four types of resistance (passive, militant, messianic, and proselytic), Revelation's is closest to the messianic, such as one finds in the Egyptian Potter's Oracle and Demotic Chronicle and the Jewish Psalms of Solomon, 11QMelchizedek, and 4 Ezra.

5. H. H. Rowley, in *The Relevance of Apocalyptic*, rev. ed. (New York: Harper & Brothers, 1946), chap. 4, "The Enduring Message of Apocalyptic," 150–78, calls for a canonical reading but seems to mean by it something other than is here suggested. For Rowley, to read Revelation canonically means to read it in light of Jesus, not in the context of scripture's narrative plot.

6. Sidney Z. Ehler, in *Twenty Centuries of Church and State* (Westminster, Md.: Newman Press, 1957), succinctly surveys the ongoing struggle of Christians with the state. A volume that offers a penetrating analysis of current issues is William Bentley Ball (ed.), *In Search of a National Morality* (San Francisco: Ignatius Press/ Grand Rapids: Baker, 1992). Two essays raise questions about analogies of our culture with that of the Apocalypse: W. B. Ball, "Intrusions upon the Sacred," 207–20 (which is frightening in its import), and Robert P. Dugan, Jr., "The Attack on Ministries," 221–31 (which is sobering, to say the least). In our culture, the first beast would be a statist government in which the state defines the good, teaches the good (as it has defined it), and enforces the good (as it has defined it). In our culture, the second beast would be the "entertainment industry/news media/educational

establishment" complex, which is engaged in social engineering in support of statist government. In our culture, Jezebel and Balaam would be the church's own salaried spokespersons who beat the drum for statist society while aggressively attacking and discounting historic Christian faith.

7. Brevard S. Childs, *The New Testament as Canon: An Introduction* (Philadelphia: Fortress, 1984), 515, says of Revelation's canonical perspective: "The supreme threat facing the world is not the possibility of a nuclear holocaust, but the absolute certainty of God's coming to judge his creation in righteousness."

8. Hal Lindsey, *The Late Great Planet Earth* (Grand Rapids: Zondervan, 1970) and John F. Walvoord, *Armageddon, Oil, and the Middle East Crisis* (Grand Rapids: Zondervan, 1974) represent what, in my opinion, is *eisegesis* (= reading one's views into) of Revelation. For the roots of modern premillenialism, see Charles C. Ryrie, *The Basis of Premillenial Faith* (Neptune, N.J.: Loizeaux Brothers, 1953).

FOR FURTHER READING

ON APOCALYPTIC

John J. Collins, ed., "Apocalypse: The Morphology of a Genre," *Semeia* 14 (1979)
This volume of *Semeia* surveys the Jewish Apocalypses, Early Christian Apocalypses, the Gnostic Apocalypses, and Greek and Latin Apocalypses, and offers the definitive morphology of the genre.

D. S. Russell, *The Method and Message of Jewish Apocalyptic, 200 B.C.–A.D. 100* (Philadelphia: Westminster Press, 1964)
Although an older treatment, it is the best single survey of the message of the apocalypses.

ON REVELATION

Research commentaries

R. H. Charles, *The Revelation of St. John*, 2 vols. (Edinburgh: T. & T. Clark, 1920)
Although its diachronic method is obsolete, it remains the single best source for useful comparative material.

H. B. Swete, *The Apocalypse of John* (London: Macmillan, 1917)
Less comparative material than Charles, but better balanced in its reading.

Mid-level commentaries

M. Eugene Boring, *Interpretation: Revelation* (Louisville: Westminster/John Knox, 1989)
A creative synthesis by a mature interpreter. It does not follow a verse-by-verse format.

Robert H. Mounce, *The Book of Revelation* (Grand Rapids: Eerdmans, 1977)
A balanced, well-informed treatment following the verse-by-verse format.

A homiletic treatment

Eugene H. Peterson, *Reversed Thunder: The Revelation of John and the Praying Imagination* (San Francisco: Harper & Row, 1988)
Its author, a Presbyterian pastor, says he reads Revelation not to get new information but to revive his imagination.